COUNTRY MATTERS

Peter Vincent

CANTERLEY
PUBLISHING

Edited by
Diana Wheeler

With assistance from
Ros Humphries and Patrick Wheeler

And made possible by generous contributions from the
Tory Family Foundation, and some private donors.

Published by Canterley Publishing
www.canterley.co.uk
info@canterley.co.uk

Printed in the United Kingdom.

ISBN-13: 978-1-9164981-4-3

First published 2020.

INTRODUCTION

For those who never knew him or do not remember him, Peter Vincent was a much-admired member of the Elham community, known for his farming in the area, but also as an Editor of the Parish Magazine for many years. His regular commentaries on the farming and natural world were enjoyed by all and revealed a charm and humour, as well as a literary ability that endeared him to his regular following.

This introduction is drawn from the recollections of a few still living in the village that knew him well, including his son Ian, Colin Johnson and Bernard Edwards. Apart from the pleasure this selection of his articles will hopefully give, they may also fulfil a long-held ambition of Peter's. As his son Ian has said, 'I believe that if he had one regret, it was that he never had the time to write the book that he had inside him'.

Peter and his siblings, Alan and Mary were born to Wilfred and Edna, née Martin, at Pound Farm, Newington. He was the third generation of the Vincent family to be farmers and his greatest passion was his dairy herd, Ayrshire cows. Peter's paternal grandfather purchased his first farm at Stelling Minnis in 1908. His farming empire grew rapidly, with various members of the Vincent family farming land from Newington up into the Elham valley. They had most of the livestock and arable crops that you would expect in this area. In particular they established the pedigree Longport Ayrshire dairy herd. Peter's maternal great grandfather was a miller whose son established a milling business - a watermill at the bottom of Horn Street, Seabrook and an engine-driven mill at Ashley Avenue, Cheriton.

Peter's primary schooling at Newington was interrupted by the Second World War when he was evacuated to his uncle's farm in Sussex. On his return to Kent he attended the Harvey Grammar School as a contemporary of Colin Johnson. Colin recalls their 'uneventful journey through secondary education, neither of us achieving major academic distinction except in two disciplines: PE and sport, where consistently over the years we were both awarded negative grades!'

However, after two years at the Kent Farming Institute Peter obtained a first class certificate and moved on to do his National Service where he became a wireless fitter in the RAF before returning to the family farm and dairy business.

Worried by the threat that the construction of the M20 and Channel Tunnel would have on the Longport herd, Peter sold Pound Farm to purchase Milldown Farm, Acryse and Water Farm, Elham, and renamed the herd as Milldown.

Peter was noted for his commitment to his local community. Bernard Edwards recalls an example of Peter's selfless and generous character in coming to the aid of a recently widowed woman who found herself with a virtually unsaleable property, half built on the old Elham station platform, as it had partially collapsed. Somehow he helped salvage the situation, and Bernard felt that his solution was a true example of his public-spirited character.

Peter was a regular at church services throughout his life at Newington and Elham. He was a social joiner, a regular meeting goer and was on many committees, many of which he chaired at some time or another. These committees included the Young Farmers club and NFU, then Newington Parish Council, Elham Parochial Church Council, and also Newington village hall committee. He was a governor of Elham Primary School.

As an active member of the Acryse Young Farmers Club, Peter often said that his greatest achievement was recruiting, courting and marrying Lynda, née Hambrook.

Peter never really retired from farming, but as he took a less hands-on role in the business, he was glad to use his natural flair for writing to edit the Elham Parish Magazine, a position he enjoyed for several years. He led a full life, later quietly studying the lives of ordinary country folk and the animals that surrounded him, and enjoying the company of his much-loved family.

He used his column 'Country Matters' to write these delightful cameos of rural life which will hopefully give readers as much pleasure as he gained from writing them.

ONE

2001

If a man write a better book, preach a better sermon, or make a better mouse-trap than his neighbour, tho' he build his house in the woods, the world will make a beaten path to his door.

Ralph Emerson

Many years ago a relative of mine drove a fairly dilapidated Toyota. He usually carried a bag of cattle feed in the boot, 'just in case'. One day, by chance, the bag he picked up contained a mouse or two. Probably two, as virgin births are not common in mice. I have heard it said, 'two's company three's a crowd'. In this instance the number of small mice rapidly exceeded crowd levels. As he drove off, the mice would emerge from cover and congregate on the top of the rear seat. By the time he reached third gear the whole family were lined up to enjoy the view only to disappear as soon as the car stopped. Had they remained, as rodents living in a bag of rolled barley, it would have been reasonably easy to apprehend the intruders. Since they only visited the bag at meal times and spent the rest of the time in the upholstery increasing their numbers, control was difficult.

By now the electrics in the car were beginning to give trouble so an anti-mouse campaign was planned. The first move was to shut a cat in the stationary car. Since the mice only came out of the upholstery to eat or enjoy the view, this had little effect. Round One to the mice! Keeping the cat in the car on its rounds raised the stakes. This was of course long before it was proposed to make hunting mice with cats illegal. The cat was so terrified by the movement that she flew round and round the car making normal driving impossible. This further upset the cat, which had a disastrous attack of diarrhoea. The driver abandoned ship, rapidly followed by the cat. The mice, thankful for the fresh air from the open door, stayed aboard. Mice Two, Driver Nil!

The next move was to remove the bag of cattle food and replace it with mouse bait. Unfortunately the mice had forestalled this move by secreting a cache of barley in the structure of the car. Others had genetically modified their dietary requirements to enable them to survive on electrical insulation. A few Kamikaze mice consumed a lethal dose of poison and died in the upholstery. Two more days and the car was replaced and downgraded to a farm run around. It was the

1

only vehicle I have ever driven which was improved by taking a very dead sheep to the kennels.

Over the past 35 years it has been my duty as a father and grandfather to read many books to many children. Some could have been classed as literature, others as rubbish. The 'tale' which follows is neither kind of fiction, it is simply a statement of fact or rather a list of facts so unlikely that, even though I have seen them unfold with my own eyes, I can scarcely believe them. By way of introduction I will mention 'The Borrowers' by Mary Norton. This is a book for children of primary school age, about creatures of human form, but of mouse size, who live in houses and the countryside. They survive by 'borrowing' all their needs from the human race. Because they always keep out of sight their depredations are blamed on mice. Fanciful you may say, but no more than most children's fiction.

In November 2000 I opened the door of my truck to see a mouse disappear behind the glove compartment. This is of course a complete misnomer as the one thing, which it does not contain, is a glove. Most other articles, which could be useful in treating a sick sheep or doing a temporary repair to machine or fence, are there, if you can find them. Memory leaped back to the tragedy of the Toyota. The two bitch collies are enthusiastic mouse hunters, but cause more damage than a whole tribe of mice. A spring trap would fly off as soon as I left the road. A special design was called for.

The basis of this trap was a 500gm margarine tub. In the top I cut two holes about an inch in diameter, just in case the guests couldn't understand metric. I filled the tub about a third full of mouse bait, fitted the lid and placed my nouveau trap in the glove compartment. Two days later I inspected my trap. There was no sign of a mouse. The level of the bait may have fallen slightly, but more interestingly the pot now contained a lump of black wool, a portion of a J cloth, part of the tray of a match box and six small rubber rings which are used for removing lambs' tails. Over the next eight weeks the level of bait continued to fall but there was nothing to indicate that it had any ill effect upon mice. The only change was an increase in their enthusiasm as collectors. At one stage one entrance was sealed with sticky tape and paper, the instructions purloined from a medicine bottle.

In the middle of January I took an inventory. In addition to the label from the bottle and an electrical screwdriver which I had retrieved for my own use, one hole was now blocked with another lump of black wool, the remains of a match box and a tube of eye ointment. The other was sealed with a spare rear light bulb. A suggestion was made that the mice needed light at night, but the bulb was fitted the wrong way round. Inside there was more black wool, the tray of the match box chewed into small pieces and a few remaining strands of a J cloth. These literary mice had also acquired two covers of a ballpoint pen, one nozzle and one ink tube. The tub contained 21 matches, 18 tailing rings, one hypodermic syringe, and two needles for it with cases. There was also a 45ml roofing nail, a nut and bolt, the nozzle from an aerosol can, a dust cap from a car tyre and two small plastic plugs.

Since my first brief encounter I have not seen another mouse or any trace of one. I am mystified as to how a mouse or even a team of mice could have manoeuvred these objects through the small entrance holes. I may have discovered from where Mary Norton got her plot, but most of all, I would like to know why a mouse or mice undertook this Herculean task. Perhaps this assortment was not being collected, but disposed of. Maybe they were telling me that the poisoned food was not appreciated, so they were filling the pot with other worthless objects, sealing the access and starting with a clean sheet. After all it is Lent. Surely this is the purpose of it. We have this opportunity to clear our minds of unnecessary clutter and concentrate on the main issue, the approach of Easter.

TWO

A LOCAL FARMER SURVEYS THE WINTER SCENE

1981

Anyone not directly involved with farming might be excused for thinking that with all the modem machinery available it is a much easier job than it used to be. It is true that we no longer sweat and toil as our grandparents did. The machine is a relentless task-master. It does not need a rest as oxen and horses do, and because we are not exhausted physically we drive ourselves and each other to work on and on. This is especially so from July to December. So I was very pleased to drill the last of the winter corn. There is of course, more to do with the stock, and we are still ploughing the rest of the land for drilling in the Spring. This is best done before Christmas to enable the frost to provide a good tilth and kill off the diseases which lay lurking in the stubbles, but once hard frosts put an

end to autumn drilling we call to a halt the four months at continual panic stations.

If I were an artist and had been commissioned to paint a scene of human helplessness and dejection, I should have been out this month with brown and grey paint in a potato field. Nothing shows better how far science has mastered nature than twenty thousand pounds worth of tractor and potato harvester up to its axles in gluey slime. Pickers, as muddy and wet as the field, fight through three coats to sort mud from spud. The monotony of the toil gives them time to think, 'As each day passes, the mud grows colder, the spuds more blighted and frosted.' A flight of duck rise up from the headland. But there is a shaft of winter sunlight in this grey scene. When science has been conquered by nature, the potato picker will rise victorious, if not phoenix-like, from the ashes, at least like a duck from the puddle.

An old dairy farmer once told me, in great disgust, of a comment made by a city dweller freshly moved to the village. 'It must be a lot easier for you farmers now that winter has come and you don't have to drive your cows to and from the pasture, twice a day'. In those days two men had to work hard twelve hours a day, seven days a week, to keep thirty cows clean, fed, milked and watered throughout the winter. Two men can care for many more cows today with piped water, tractor-fed silage and mechanised waste disposal, but there is still much more hard work in caring for a herd in winter than the summer. Even dairy men like to have some time off at Christmas so we try to work shifts. If the weather is mild we can cope with the necessary work and still have a break, but I for one have nightmares about a white Christmas. The card scenes never show the frozen water pipes, thirsty cattle and stranded milk tankers. The grasses which are grown on farms today are carefully bred to give high yields of nutritious feed to the animals. Unfortunately, some have lost the natural hardiness of their ancestors. Just as modern civilised man would find it difficult to survive in the stone age, so hybrid grasses need special treatment to survive the winter. Farmers who keep sheep will have their leys grazed down tight before the hard frosts, and searing north-east winds can burn off the lush top. Dairy farmers often borrow a flock of sheep for this task.

Thus, what helps the shepherd to see the sheep safely through the winter also protects the cows' food for next summer. The husbandry we have developed through the ages has been complete and interdependent, with each part helping to support the whole. If because of greed, hunger or economic pressure we upset the balance by greatly increasing one crop at the expense of another, we must be very careful that we are not starting downhill on a dangerous helterskelter which can have no end but bankruptcy of the soil, our most valuable capital asset.

THREE

A FAIRY TALE FOR CHRISTMAS

1981

How long is a piece of string? How many loaves, for that matter sausages, are equal to a barrel of oil? I once heard an old Sussex farmer answer the first question – From 'ere t'other end', and the same answer would apply equally well to a string of sausages. The answer is infinitely variable according to how the sausages are produced, but for each string there is an answer, albeit unknown. Once upon a time the answer was infinity.

A herd of pigs wandered in woods around Elham, growing fat on beech nuts and acorns. A few strayed towards Barham Downs and were devoured by bears. Mostly they survived until December when they were killed and eaten by the good folk of Elham for their Christmas dinner; then they all lived happily ever after, except of course, for the 80% who died young of the plague or were drowned when the Nailbourne flooded. Then came the Industrial Revolution. The good fairy, called 'science', waved her magic wand, the plague vanished and we learnt how to control the environment until, like the old woman who lived in a shoe, Elham had so many children she didn't know what to do. Unlike her predecessor, she did not give them some bread, for there wasn't enough to share. Instead she sent them all over the world to fill up the empty spaces and teach the local inhabitants how they could use the good fairy's magic to increase and multiply.

With all these babies being born and growing up, there were soon no empty spaces left and not enough woods for the pigs to roam in. Once again the good fairy waved her wand. She said 'I will show you how to eat the horrible black sludge that oozes from the earth so that no one need be hungry'. Then the good fairy showed the farmers how to use fertiliser made from oil so instead of growing one ton of barley per acre they could grow two or even three tons. The pigs were taken from the woods and shut in environmentally controlled houses heated with more oil and fed on barley until the sausages stretched from dawn to sunset. Still the mouths could not be filled. Then the good fairy told the farmers that it was not necessary to rotate their crops as their ancestors had done ever since they first settled in the Elham Valley. She told them to slaughter the stock which manured their land and grow just wheat and barley to provide more food. Some of the farmers were very unhappy about this, but the good fairy put a spell on them and called them reactionaries, so no one listened to them. When all the weeds, insects and fungi which devastate cereals saw that there were no more break crops they found they could increase and multiply even more rapidly than the people of Elham had done. Once again the people felt starvation. They cried for help to the good fairy who answered, 'If you wish I will take more oil and give you "cides" to protect your crops'.

So she took more oil and made herbicides, fungicides and pesticides. Now the farmers could grow four tons of wheat and barley per acre. Eventually there came a time when there was so much oil being used to produce a sausage that some people said they could actually taste it. They forgot that if it hadn't been for the good fairy, their grandparents would have starved and they would never have been born. Some said the good fairy was really a wicked witch in disguise, trying to poison the people with her magic and that the farmers were her allies. This was really very rude, for you should never criticise a farmer with your mouth full. The good fairy was tired and cross. She said, 'I have used up all my spells feeding your ever-increasing family. I have but one more "cide". If you do not learn to control your numbers before my magic oil runs dry, I can only offer suicide.'

FOUR

1991

Your scalds still thunder and prophesy
That crown that never comes;
Friend I will watch the certain things,
Swine and slow moons like silver rings,
And the ripening of the plums.

G.K. Chesterton

I drove through Newington today. Three years ago I made this trip every day and enjoyed it, but for the last two years I have avoided it when I could. Like 'Sweet Auburn' it has become a deserted village. Well, not so much deserted as devoid of village life, though the meadows where 'the sober herd once lowed to meet their young' now resound to more Irish voices than Auburn in her heyday.

To me these were never just meadows, part of a beautiful landscape but, as part of my childhood, so part of me. The little pond where the willows bent low to form giant fishing rods and moorhen chicks bobbed like corks then hid where leaves and water met, was never just a pretty pond. That was the pond where my sister and I tried to taste the forbidden fruit, or rather pick a kingcup at the water's edge, and struggled from the mud, much later, much dirtier and minus marsh marigold and boots, to receive a very long lecture on the dangers of playing near water, and the cost of two pairs of boots. Now it is a desert of wet sand. There was a culvert that led the drains under the railway embankment. Sitting in the grass, aged about five, waiting for the train to pass, I met my first fox. I must say he behaved like a perfect gentleman and didn't bat a whisker as he disappeared down the culvert. Having been reared on a literary diet of Little Red Riding Hood, I let out a scream which probably drowned the whistle of the approaching train and headed to home as fast as two short fat legs would allow. Now there is no culvert because there is no embankment and no first primroses growing in this sheltered south-facing spot; primroses which could only be picked by reaching an arm through the railway fence. We knew that to put one foot through the fence was to face certain death from the train which would instantly appear, derail and crush us.

Pound Farm was probably the only farm in Kent which had a camel. What a pity more people did not realise this. In this conservation conscious age it must have been seen as an endangered species and become the subject of a preservation order.

190 years ago the Prince Regent applied the royal seal to the General Enclosure Act effectively putting an end to the old open field system of farming in southern and eastern England. The new enclosures were to be the salvation of British agriculture. The Rigden family, who farmed Pound Farm, worked hard for long hours planting hawthorn hedges and digging ditches to divide the farm into neat rectangular fields of convenient size. The farm prospered. Then came the forties and the repeal of the Corn Laws. There was no way to make ends meet competing with wheat grown on the virgin soils of the New World. The farm changed hands. For the next fifty years it was run as a dairy farm by the Graves family. The heavy gault clay made rich fertile pasture, the thick hawthorn hedges provided shelter for one of the best shorthorn herds in the country with Folkestone a ready market for the milk and cream. Once again it was not the farming which went wrong but the circumstances which changed. One hundred years ago the railway was driven diagonally through the farm to 'bring prosperity to Folkestone and revitalise the whole Elham Valley'. The economical rectangular fields, once the pride of the farm, became awkward triangular patches. Many fields had no water or difficult access so cows were allowed to wander at will. No one bothered to lay the once neat hedges which became stunted trees with gaps between them and no economic purpose. The ponds were allowed to silt up, dried out in summer and were surrounded with marshy areas in winter.

One particular hawthorn had been laid as a young tree and ran horizontally for about four feet. Twice in its first hundred years it had rebelled against this unnatural position and sent a branch soaring to the sky, but each time this unruly behaviour had been checked by a Rigden blade. Each time the wound had healed

leaving a lump on the prostrate trunk. By the third attempt the hedge was no longer needed as a cattle barrier so the twisted tree was allowed the extravagance of lifting its head to the sky. By the time I met this particular hawthorn it was about one hundred and fifty years old, its head crowned with a mass of blossom in May to be followed by scarlet berries in autumn. It had thrown down suckers below the crown and appeared to be galloping through the meadow shaking an imperious head on a long neck in defiance of the world. Above all the two humps on its back would prove to any imaginative five-year old that this was a camel. From that day I had an escape from the problems of childhood. I had only to trot two hundred yards to the camel and, squeezing lightly between the front hump and the bark-encrusted neck I could ride away to a land where no one worried if you were late for school, where shoelaces tied themselves, where sums always added up and everyone ate apple pie and condensed milk all the time. The camel was not just my friend. Younger members of my family, nieces and nephews, my children and their friends all rode away to their dreams on the camel. In death the camel must feel truly at home for the spot where he once galloped is now covered by a lump of concrete the size of a small pyramid. In 1808 William Cobbett was thundering against the enclosure act which took away the independence of the countryman. No doubt the Graves family felt pretty strongly about the railway which cut through their farm, for many of them emigrated to Canada. One could see at our Parish Outing how many men regret the passing of steam and I, like Cobbett, must be allowed to regret the transition from agriculture to industry. I don't doubt that in another hundred years, when the tunnel no longer serves a useful purpose, some sentimentalist will mourn its passing.

FIVE

1991

His name I know, and what his trumpet saith.
Whether man's heart or life it be which yields
Thee harvest, must Thy harvest fields
Be dunged with rotten death?

Francis Thompson

Passing the time of day with an elderly gardener some years ago, I mentioned that I had heard a suggestion that the date of Easter should be fixed. This did not seem to interest him, but five minutes later he suddenly asked, 'What about Good Friday?' 'What about Good Friday? I replied. 'Are they going to muck about with that date then?' I opined that you couldn't have Easter without Good Friday. 'T'wont work', he stated, 'T'aint natural'. A couple of beers later I discovered the root of the problem. He always planted his potatoes on Good Friday. How could this work if Good Friday was fixed? It couldn't allow for an early spring or a late one. It seemed prudent to move on so I suggested that civil servants couldn't be expected to have sufficient common sense to understand the problem and we parted in total accord.

Personally, I never plant potatoes on Good Friday as I am too preoccupied with lambs. Since lambs fill my life throughout Easter, I no longer plant potatoes at all which is probably a pity since the potato realistically paints a far better picture of Easter than a lamb. There is no better symbol of Easter than a shrivelled old potato which is placed in the ground on Good Friday to rot and emerge as a vital plant resurrected through decay. Compare this to a lamb, which strenuously fights against my pulling to bring it into the world, sullenly resists my efforts to persuade it to breathe, instantly finds reverse gear when a teat is placed in its mouth and spends the rest of its life discovering ways of flouting my attempts to protect it from disaster.

Surely sheep and turkeys have a special genius for seeking an untimely demise. In spite of this, or perhaps because of this, I have never lost my enthusiasm for lambing. I once heard someone ask the son of a shepherd if he loved seeing the lambs born. With typical teenage bravado he replied he had seen so many lambs born he was tired of the sight of birth. I hope he was showing off, if not I pity

him. When one is bored by birth and death there can be little joy in life. There are times when through consistently broken nights and early mornings, through days fighting against wind and rain and failure, we believe we are totally exhausted. At such a time visitors often arrive and ask to see a lamb born. Then we find a sheep in trouble and if we can manage to sort out the tangle of twelve legs twisted up in the dark recesses of the ewe and, one by one, deliver three live lambs with the panache of a conjuror pulling a rabbit from a hat and watch the wonder in the children's faces, then we know why we continue to farm. These mysteries and the joy of observing and discovering the secrets of the countryside in the course of a working day, compensate for the lack of sleep and regular days off.

I was feeding a yard of cattle one morning when out of the corner of my eye I noticed violent movement among their legs. My first thought was that one had calved, but looking more closely, I could see that a life and death struggle was taking place. A hawk had dropped amongst the cattle to seize one of the flock of starlings who sift through the straw for the odd grain of barley which combine and cattle have missed. Although the starling was a large quarry the struggle did not last long. The hawk wings were the only ones to move as they rose in the air. I felt a certain empathy with the predator as I had to leave and select a load of lambs. Lambs which six months earlier I had coaxed into life I now had to select for slaughter, but farmers, like hawks, have to eat to live.

This morning, I had a totally different experience of rebirth. After driving through unploughed snow, a foot deep, to feed sheep on Running Hill, I paused to look into the valley. Elham had vanished. A new village had appeared in the night, perhaps like Brigadoon for just one day in one hundred years, and I was the privileged one to gaze on its pristine glory. No footstep or wheel track blemished the unbroken surface. White rooves contrasted with the dark shadows of walls and chimney pots. No movement broke the spell of total unreality. Was this the clean slate the world was awaiting? Next week, I shall look down on slush and mud, old blemishes will reappear and I shall long for the glimmer of spring to colour all green, but for today, I rejoice at the vision of the valley in white.

Yesterday, at dusk, as I passed a window, a movement in the middle of a field caught my eye. Two dark figures were cavorting in the unsullied snow. I seized a pair of binoculars and discovered they were hares behaving in true March fashion a month before time. One was burrowing in the snow until only its ears were visible and then leaped out, as if to surprise the other which all the while had been racing round in circles. The game was repeated again and again until bad light stopped play. I shall never know if this was a courtship ritual or sheer joie de vivre because they, like me, were fascinated by this strange new world. I can never begrudge them the little circles which they eat in the corn, they are such superb entertainment value with their irrational extrovert behaviour. Hares have a special message for those of us who become so involved with the business of living that we cannot find time to live. They are far too busy enjoying life to do more than token damage to a crop. It is their cousins the rabbits who consistently maximise their opportunities and so frequently destroy the environment on which they depend. That I suppose is why rabbits are so popular in fiction, they are so very human.

SIX

1991

In this age of high priced beef,
Little lard and bits of bacon.
When an old cow comes to grief
Where is her cold body taken?
Embodiment of skin and grief,
Cast aside that look of sorrow,
Burghers passing all belief
You shall be this time tomorrow

I can remember a time when there were five Ayrshire herds in the Elham Valley; now there are only six in Kent and Essex. Those of us who still keep the breed, or are otherwise attached to it, have formed a club which meets to inspect the herds, exchange information and socialise with other breeders. This spring it was our turn to act as hosts. For two days before the visit my wife lapsed into a catering frenzy whilst I reminded her there are no longer fifty Ayrshire breeders in the south east. I walked around in small circles wondering when the farm became so untidy and hampered the clean-up by sending everyone in three directions at once, whilst senior son demanded a decision on Natasha. Natasha is a lady of late middle age who has, for the past six years, made a substantial contribution to our milk quota. She has true Prima Donna temperament and in her earlier years perfected a scything swing of the leg which would remove a milking machine and a milker's equanimity with one blow. Of late she has become much easier to live with. Last year, as soon as she was in calf, she started to limp. Toenail trimming and a search for stones or foot rot produced no results, so the vet was called in to make the diagnosis which we refused to consider.

'We've trimmed her feet but she still seems tender - Muscle looks a bit wasted - She milks too well to carry much flesh - Could just be a touch of arthritis.' At last the dread words are out.

For cows there is no youth restoring hip replacement; just a slow decline until the slaughter house becomes the more merciful option. There is no room for sentimentality in farming, and I am well used to selecting young steers, lambs or cockerels to grace a table, but an old cow is different. We have shared many hours in the milking parlour, and I can easily forget how hard was her hoof. Now if she kicked it would hurt her more than me. Since Murphy's Law dictates that arthritis is only diagnosed when a cow is just in calf she is automatically granted nine months stay of execution. Then we decide to keep her for a few months to build her up after calving. The better the cow the bigger the percentage of food which produces milk and the less is left for flesh. Trying to fatten an arthritic Natasha is like pumping up a tyre with a very fast puncture. 'We could turn her down Sandbanks and not bother to take them down there' says the siren voice of temptation. 'No, leave her with the herd', I decide hoping that one lean cow will disappear amongst the plump eighty nine, although I know in my heart that Pharaoh dreamt it right and one lean cow can hide seven fat ones any day. Ultimately our visitors are too polite to ask why we have kept that awful screw, confirming what I suspected. They have all had their moment of truth and kept their Natasha too long.

Of course, breeds of cow are not the only things that have changed dramatically in farming over the past fifteen years. Long before man first walked upright or wondered where he came from, before he had the energy or strength to reproduce or consider where the species was going to, his primary objective was to fill his belly. The basic need remained the same from Genesis to the nineteen seventies. Of course, as we became civilised we learnt how to consume much more than we could produce by beggaring others whilst others learnt how to live without producing. One hundred and fifty years ago my great great grandfather could not afford horses, but food was needed, so he yoked his donkey and bull together and ploughed the Sussex Weald. Farmers knew where they were going, they were going to produce more food for an ever-increasing demand.

When I moved to Elham fourteen years ago I was given a grant to go into milk production because the EEC was short of dairy produce. Six years later I was told to cut production by ten per cent. Natasha and her colleagues don't respond to EEC directives so the alternative was to slaughter 10% of the herd. We used the surplus grass for sheep production. Now we are told to cut lamb and wool as well as cereals, oil seed and beef. Suddenly, after the progress of thousands of years farming does not know where it is going. Some politicians suggest that farmers should be paid to maintain a green and pleasant environment. If the community wishes to employ me as a park keeper or gardener I have no objection to the principle. It sounds preferable to being selected as one of the 10% surplus to requirements. I have yet to be convinced that the real problem is over production rather than under distribution.

There are said to be 27 million people in Africa in danger of starvation. Millions of Kurds and Bangladeshis can be added to the total and further victims of war, weather and poverty increase the number daily. I accept that the only viable long term solution is to provide a peaceful environment and assist these people to produce their own food, but this will not happen this year or next. There will be no long term for the stick-limbed swollen-bellied children we see each night on television if we do not provide sufficient short term aid. The need is too large for voluntary organisations to fill. The biggest problem facing EEC ministers is to come to agreement with the GATT negotiators. I know it would not be easy to shift the food from our stores to the famine areas. It would cost a vast amount of money to give it away. Distributing it would require a lot of imagination and problems would arise. Are these difficulties really beyond the ability of governments which recently mounted operation 'Desert Storm'? Might it not be easier to live with the problem of saving life than taking it? Should we not look upon our stores as a strategic reserve rather than a surplus? The idea is not new. 3,600 years ago the Egyptians stored their surplus for seven years and helped their starving neighbours when famine struck. Has civilisation really morally impoverished us so much over that period?

Storing temporary surplus is a solution adopted by many species. We have an old collie named Podger who spends most of his waking hours searching for any scraps or carrion which he buries behind the boiler shed. I cannot work out whether he is public-spirited or stupid as he never benefits from his thrift. If he hides anything that is worth eating it is disinterred by the younger collies. Last week, senior son returned from a shopping trip to hear the telephone ringing. Leaving one of his bags on the doorstep, he rushed in to answer it. Returning twenty minutes later he found an empty bag. Round the corner Podger was busily covering a very dirty salami sausage. I don't know who eventually ate the sausage but Podger received a large boot in a soft place for coming between son and salami. Perhaps similar treatment should be meted out to politicians who believe surplus food should be stored until it decomposes.

SEVEN

1991

Know all ye sheep
And cows that keep
On staring that I stand so long
In grass that's wet from heavy rain -
A rainbow and a cuckoo's song
May never come together again

William Henry Davies

I was walking through a field of wheat last summer, hoping to mark out a footpath which was in danger of becoming overgrown, followed by two collies. I noticed the wheat to my right was waving as though a mini whirlwind was building up. I told the dogs to sit and walked slowly towards the disturbance, expecting to surprise a rabbit or a hare. It was not the cause of the unrest, but me who was surprised when I came face to face, or rather jaw to leg with a large badger. I had never been in such close proximity to a live badger and wasn't quite certain how I should behave. Brock evidently felt the same as for several minutes neither of us moved a muscle. Having observed as much badger as I could I remembered that Ben could not be relied upon to sit much longer, that I had a large expanse of bare leg between shorts and shoes and in my mind's eye could see the damage that badger claws could inflict on a henhouse door. I decided on a tactical withdrawal. I watched from a distance but saw no movement in the wheat so left well satisfied that the two most powerful free mammals on Milldown had succeeded in communicating that neither had any aggressive intentions towards the other.

Speaking later to one of our local police force, he told me that when he came to the area, whilst driving round the lanes at night, he would frequently see a fox but a badger was a rarity. Now the badger is the more common of the two. This is also the experience of our family. One night I was driving an elderly relative home after a family wedding. My passenger had dozed off in the back seat but was rudely awakened when a badger decided to test my brakes by jumping into the lane in front of me and running for about twenty yards before turning up a well-worn path and under the hedge, leaving me with no evidence or excuse for tipping a sleeping passenger into the foot well.

I believe these tracks are even older than the manmade roads they cross, but unfortunately the badger's insistence on his right of way can cause a breakdown in communications. The daughter of a neighbour was out on an early morning ride when she found badger caught in a snare. She rode home and told her father that he had to do something quickly. Quite prepared to put an injured animal out of its pain, he reached for his gun but this approach was speedily dismissed. He was told he had to mount a rescue operation. Daughter led the way to the scene followed by father and a reluctant mother armed with a pair of thick gauntlets, a broom and a pair of wire cutters.

Plan A was for mother in road to distract the badger with the broom whilst daughter in field held the wire for father to cut. The only success of this scheme was to shorten the broom handle and further enrage the badger who was none too pleased to start with. Seeking inspiration, mother felt in her pockets, produced the dog's choke chain and, with great panache, lassoed the badger. It was now a simple task for father and daughter to cut the snare free. The only problem now was that mother had a very cross badger on a very short choke chain. The only way the badger could move was forward, which he did. Mother decided she didn't really need the choke chain which was removed by father with a deft flick of a very short broom. As Brock charged through the hedge, mother sprinted down the lane out of harm's way, unfortunately, in the direction of the badger track which is just the way a frightened badger will run. Looking over her shoulder she saw Brock hard on her heels and kicked into overdrive with an ear-piercing yell. For a short while it was touch and go which would break Christie's hundred metre time first but eventually the badger nosed ahead and mother collapsed on the bank white and shaking and very indignant at the lack of sympathy from hysterical husband and daughter.

+++++

We share Milldown Farm with three cats. Tumbleweed, the youngest and most aggressive, loves the lambing season and is our constant companion in the lambing shed which provides excellent mousing. She was sitting on the edge of a pen which housed one ewe with a new lamb, waiting for a rustle in the straw to solidify into a mouse, when the ewe decided she constituted a threat to the lamb. One hundred and forty pounds of sheep hurled herself at four pounds of cat to be greeted by a mighty smack on the nose with unsheathed claws. The ewe retreated with her lamb to the far corner of the pen having understood the message that it was Tumbleweed's pen and sheep were only allowed in on Tumbleweed's terms. I think we probably have the only sheep-worrying cat in the county.

We had a sick sheep the other day who was unable to feed her lambs. Hoping she would recover we decided to supplement their diet with a bottle. One accepted this arrangement readily but not so the other. The more we chased him the more terrified he became. Exhausted and in desperation whilst feeding the tame lamb I dropped on hands and knees and mimicked the mother's bleat. To my amazement the lamb came running to me, seized the proffered bottle and commenced drinking. My wife, who was falling about laughing, threatened to video me with my foster baby but why should I worry? If you think it's the first time a Peter has been ridiculed for communicating across the language barrier try reading Acts 2 Verse 13.

EIGHT

1991

Where have all our 'turtles' gone?

edited by Peter Vincent

The swallows will soon be back with a noisy flutter round their old patch excitedly inspecting the buildings, the rooves, the perching wires and even their old nests, all in the first few minutes of their arrival. After the smug pleasure of being the first to hear the cuckoo we all thrill to hear the unmistakeable chorus from deep in the bushes confirming the return of our elusive nightingales.

Summer's approach is confirmed when the cheerful little turtle doves arrive. They are the smallest dove of our five species, about the size of a blackbird and the only one which regularly migrates, spending the winter south of the Sahara and returning in early May to live on weed seeds, grain and some vegetation, quite often raising two broods of twins in a flat nest made of twigs usually in tall thick hedgerows.

Unfortunately, I am remembering the past when swallows nested in nearly every farm building and followed the mowing machines in whirling flocks snatching 'Meadow Browns' from the clouds of disturbed butterflies, soaring up to nibble a mouthful and swooping down to catch the falling pieces.

I am remembering the days when families of screaming house martins filled the street in front of the Yew Tree Inn. Nightjars 'churred' continuously all night in the totally cleared Abbots Wood. Corncrakes could still be seen on Endlewick Farm and occasionally buzzards from Birling Gap soared around Underwood. Song thrushes cracked snail shells open on their favourite stone in the corner of most country gardens. Local people actually complained that the chorus of countless nightingales kept them awake at night and in those days only forty or fifty years ago, pairs of turtle doves cooed and purred in nearly every hedgerow, climbing and falling in and out of their leafy sanctuary.

Farmers using modern farming methods producing enough to feed the ever-rising world population, still hungry despite regional surpluses, are blamed for the sad depletion of most of our birds by the extensive use of herbicides, pesticides and fertilisers and are accused of removing ancient hedgerows, destroying the nesting sites of many species. As a farmer I cannot deny that these necessary modern methods have changed the countryside and must have had a detrimental effect on our bird population, especially certain species, but there is still ample food and plenty of cover for nesting to support a far greater population of the very species that used to be so numerous. So where have they gone?

From personal disturbing experience I feel sure that one answer can be found along the Mediterranean coast during March and April and again in September and October where the migrating journeys of birds in their thousands come to an abrupt end in a trap or net or shot out of the sky by 'hunters' for the sheer 'joy' of shooting. The song birds are trapped and sold to spend the rest of their lives in very small cages, but other species are shot to prove the 'hunter's' skill and manhood.

During a short stay in Malta during March we were shocked to witness this annual carnage. Any waste ground has a set up with one or two 'trappers' settled in a small shelter waiting for the arrival of the migrants. Each 'trapper' places song birds in tiny cages on stone walls and rocks right round his trapping area. We saw chaffinches, goldfinches, greenfinches, linnets and serins, but we are told that hawfinches and other rare species are also used. These innocent collaborators twitter away, happy to have the covers removed from their tiny cages. Their happy songs attract the arriving migrants who settled on a big ground-coloured net in front of the shelter and are instantly caught when the 'trapper' pulls a connected cord.

Not only did we see this depressing spectacle on every available patch, but we also witnessed gangs and individual 'hunters' shooting most other species and particularly house martins that were just beginning to arrive from Africa. Our host told us that when a 'hunter' was asked why he did not shoot clay pigeons he exclaimed 'But, I do, I love it.' 'Then why do you still shoot house martins' he was asked, 'To keep in practice', he boasted. Our host was also surprised that we had seen three seagulls. 'Why shouldn't we see seagulls round an island in the Mediterranean?' we asked 'Because the hunters have shot them all' was the unfortunate answer.

When we were in Malta I was lucky to see a hoopoe, a lovely bird which we have seen in France and Spain, but they sometimes get as far as the south of England. One hot summer in the early forties I had the unforgettable thrill to see one which stayed around Sessingham Farm for two or three days. Since our return we have heard from our host that although hoopoes are now not very common, a 'hunter' has achieved a triple success and has had the honour of a photograph in the local paper to prove his skill showing three dead hoopoes. There are laws in Malta which make it illegal to shoot certain species at certain times in certain places, but even these inadequate laws are not enforced and will never be until there is a change of attitude amongst the people with the power to stop this deliberate carnage.

A top Maltese politician in a speech addressing a conference on 'Free Time, Culture and Sport' was reported in the Maltese press as saying the following: 'Many youths, who are themselves hunters or trappers are free of other temptations. Other youths appear to love animals more than they love themselves, their health and the health of others as they themselves fall victims of drugs and other vices.' What a load of political waffle! To put the tragedy into

perspective, remember that Malta is quite a small island and not on the main migration routes of our summer visitors, but most other Mediterranean countries, on the most important routes, are practising the same carnage twice every year.

Before you reach for pen and paper, finally let me say, 'Yes, I am concerned about the plight of the Kurds, the Palestinians, the Ethiopians, the Sudanese and all other human suffering all over the world, but none of these tragedies excuse the annual carnage that takes place along the flight paths of migrating birds. The following figures are from a table of birds shot and trapped annually, published in a well-respected Bird Guide and calculated by reputable ornithological organisations in Malta:

ANNUALLY SHOT AND TRAPPED

Turtle doves - up to 280,000 shot and up to another 40,000 trapped.
Cuckoos (Bee eaters and hoopoes) - 8000 (shot in approx. equal numbers)
Swifts, swallows and martins - Hard to estimate but almost certainly in excess of 40,000. All shot for fun.
Nightjars - up to 8,000
Thrushes (mostly song thrushes) - up to 300,000
Finches - Caught in large numbers which may exceed 1.5 million.

The list continues and don't forget this is just Malta.

NINE

1991

The gale, it plies the saplings double,
It blows so hard, 'twill soon be gone:
Today the Roman and his trouble
Are ashes under Uricon.

A.E. Housman

So it blew one October evening as I set out for Wick Farm to meet Mr and Mrs Ken Beeching to learn something of the secrets which they had wrested from the soil over the past 40 years. Yes, I handled a delicately engraved marble, the prized trinket of a Roman citizen which he lost on Standard Hill nearly two thousand years past. I heard how a cremation urn had been uncovered whilst digging a hole for a gate post. An urn which contained the ashes of a traveller who was walking these hills when Jesus walked in Galilee. To me, this was magic, a trip in a time capsule to the beginning of history but to Ken these things were of little consequence, just happenings of the recent past.

Ken passed me a pear-shaped lump of flint. One end was round, the size of a small cricket ball, the other chipped to form a chisel. The round end fitted neatly in my hand and I was shown how, with a chopping motion of the fore-arm, this Palaeolithic hand axe could be used to dismember a carcase. The axe I could grasp, but my mind boggled at the date, two hundred thousand years BC. The room grew misty as I pictured a small group of naked figures, crouched over a carcase, cutting off lumps of meat and carrying them off into the darkness. Is that how long man has lived in the hills that I call home? How insignificant my half century becomes.

The next implements were longer, narrower and lighter than the hand axe. These were Thames Picks used, probably by the women, for digging small animals from their burrows, but also to excavate roots which provided a dietary variation. One pick did not feel comfortable in my right hand so I transferred it to my left. I commented that even in those times some people must have been left-handed. 'Yes' replied Ken, 'the archaeologists can tell which by the scratch marks on their teeth'. This led me to muse on the problems of survival. When the whole group was involved in obtaining sufficient food to survive there was no dentist to turn to, even a minor injury could lead to starvation. The family group must have cared for the young, did they also support the old? We think of these people as

backward, sub-human, but how long would the average PhD last, deposited in the tundra with nothing but a cloak of skin, a flint hand axe and a wooden spear. Each age has its problems, they certainly did not have food mountains nor did they need a Channel Tunnel. With Britain still joined to the continent they could walk to Calais for a day's hunting. We have won so much as we have conquered the environment, but nothing comes for nothing.

We moved on a hundred thousand years to flakes of flint used as scrapers and knives. Chips skilfully broken from a lump of flint, the working edge still sufficiently sharp to cut string or scrape wood, the reverse 'retouched' or blunted to protect the user's hand. Many of these flakes, only an inch or two in diameter, were knapped so fine as to be translucent. Examples of these had been found all over Standard Hill, Wick and the surrounding farms indicating continuous habitation. I was shown how to distinguish between a naturally occurring flake and a man-made flake by the bulb of percussion where the manufactured article had been struck and how to identify the more recent finer blades which had been used for engraving. Some of these had semi-circular indentations which had been used as a spokeshave for shaping wood, bone or antlers. With the coming of the New Stone Age the craftsmanship became even more sophisticated.

I handled the heads of three maces, probably a chief's symbol of authority. One of these had been made of stone which came from the Lizard. It was beautifully rounded with a perfectly symmetrical hole through the centre to hold a wooden hasp. At the time when the Israelites were fleeing from Pharaoh there was trade throughout the breadth of Britain and skills far superior to any I would have supposed. Finally, I was shown two flint arrowheads about an inch long, one in the shape of a minute laurel leaf, the other triangular, tanged and barbed. Highly polished and translucent they revealed the beautiful veining of the flint.

I left my hosts feeling rather humble that I had been walking on so much history which I had failed to perceive and grateful for the lesson which had taught me a new respect for our distant ancestors.

TEN

ROOKS AND FIELD NAMES

1992

In 1701 Jethro Tull invented the seed drill and life has never been quite the same since. That is not until 1992. It did not really save much time to plough a field, harrow and drill it, compared with the old way of scattering beans on the stubble and ploughing them in. The big advantage was that the beans grew in rows so as they grew the whole village could turn out to hoe out the weeds. With less weeds, the fields grew more beans and so everyone had more to eat and they all lived happily ever after. It did not matter that the rooks found it much easier to pull out the shallow drilled beans than the deep ploughed ones. There were always one or two poor families in the village with plenty of children who were pleased to work all day for a few pence as 'rook starvers'. The rook population never grew out of hand because no self-respecting countryman would see spring slide by without at least one good feed of rook pie, this being in the bad old days before Tesco invented French free-range fowls. It takes five fledgling rooks and a half pound of beefsteak to make one rook pie, according to Mrs Beeton's *Compendium of Good Housekeeping*, so the balance of nature was maintained throughout the eighteenth and nineteenth centuries.

Now we are in the twentieth century everyone is well educated, wealthy and well fed, so nobody hoes for a living. It is against the law to employ children of ten to starve rooks or perform any other tasks and I am certain there is an EEC directive banning rook pie. The absence of cheap and willing hoers is generally overcome by the use of sprays, but the rook population is increasing alarmingly. Last year, they completely cleared half a field of my beans, the half out of shot gun range of the farm buildings. This year the wheel has turned full circle and we have scattered beans on the stubble and ploughed them in as our ancestors did three hundred years ago. Hopefully, they are buried too deep for the rooks to find and as the soil warms they will grow so quickly that most of them will grow through the rook barrier, but I'm hedging my bets with a few strategically placed bird scarers. Since we cannot use chemical sprays on our organic beans, we will harrow them when the crop is well established. Last year, second son came back to say I had better come and see what was happening as the harrows were pulling out the beans. Afraid of losing my nerve I told him I would rather not see, but go and finish the field. The beans recovered and most of the annual weeds were killed. The thistles are not so easy, organic farming today has certain problems which did not exist in the economic climate three hundred years ago.

+++++

Ask any visitor to Milldown to name one of the cows and you will probably receive the answer 'Wanda'. Milldown Wanda is not the most prolific milker and her love of food, and its effect on her figure, rule her out as a show cow. She is however most affectionate, particularly if you happen to have a handful of barley meal in your pocket. She is more than happy to give rides, to be cuddled by children or allow budding milkers to practise on her. Two years ago Wanda produced a daughter who needed a name beginning with 'W' after her mother. After some thought, senior son, who considers himself the literary expert of the family, pronounced the name to be 'Wordsworth', 'didn't he write something about 'Wanda'd lonely as a cloud?'. With such a launch it is not surprising that the daughter is developing into a heifer of independent spirit.

One of my Christmas presents this year was a dictionary of field names. It is a pity that with the urbanisation of society so many of these names are being lost, they have so many secrets to reveal. One of our field names, which is not in the dictionary, is 'Adam and Eve'. This is the steep bank at the top of the hill to the east of Cherry Gardens. It acquired the name from two trees which had once stood on the hill as far as anyone could remember, dating back to the days of Eden.

Last autumn I had a phone call from one of Elham's patriarchs who felt it a shame that Adam and Eve should fall into oblivion and offered to provide two youthful replacements. Of course, I jumped at this offer and Elham's own arboriculturist was commissioned to plant them. Unfortunately, he did not realise he was taking on the assistance of Beltring Connaught, Milldown Wordsworth and their friends who lost no time in assembling to enjoy the ceremony. One of the company decided it would be much more fun to see a man dig a hole without a spade so she seized it in her teeth and set off up the hill. Fortunately, it is fairly difficult for a two year-old Ayrshire heifer to run with a spade between her front legs so she was soon overhauled and dispossessed and the holes were duly dug. The first beech was planted, but the second had disappeared. I suppose one shouldn't be surprised at an Ayrshire heifer wanting to enact 'Macbeth' for there was Wordsworth leading her army along the skyline camouflaged by 'Birnam Wood' or rather the missing beech. By the time the sapling had been recovered and planted the four-wheel drive pick-up, which had been borrowed for the occasion, had started to move at first almost imperceptibly downhill. The hill is steep and tyre traction not infallible so a rapid reconnaissance was made. It was not

Banquo's ghost but three quarters of a ton of Hereford bull, by the name of Beltring Connaught, who had discovered that the back of the truck was just the same height as the itch on his shoulder. Although Connaught is the most amiable of creatures he does have a persistent streak so the wisest course seemed to be to withdraw while the truck was still intact. The new Adam and Eve should enhance the valley for many years to come and we owe our thanks to both the provider and the planter. I hope the trees live for many years as I doubt if I could persuade anyone to undertake their replacement.

ELEVEN

KANGAROO MICE AND MAIZE

1992

Lent, literally Spring, the most undisciplined adolescent of seasons, and yet, we are told, the time when we should practice self-discipline. Not a virtue which nature expects her children to possess but rather imposes her own restrictions of climate and season, bounty and shortage, seed time and harvest. It is not in evidence at 8am in the morning at Milldown. The airbrakes of the milk tanker can be heard from all round the farm buildings and are greeted by twelve canine ears springing to attention. By the time the tanker has reversed to the farm vat and the vacuum pipe is attached, 24 canine feet form a semi-circular guard of honour. As the last of the milk is drawn into the tanker, with a loud slurp, six pink tongues appear in anticipation of the pint of milk which will run from the pipe as the driver detaches it. It was Podger, the eldest of the collies who first volunteered his services as a concrete cleaning specialist and, though his legs are now no match for those of the all-consuming pair, Bella and Becky, the driver always waits until he is in position before releasing the milk.

I grew up in an old farmhouse where mice were not infrequent companions. They were grey and scuttled round skirting boards. They annoyed my mother and were caught in traps. Later I discovered they spoilt food but compensated for this by startling visiting girlfriends into one's protective arms. Other than this they were a confounded nuisance and caused much damage to the farm. It was not until I moved to Milldown that I discovered mice were not just mice. The Milldown, or Kangaroo mice, as we called them, were not grey and did not scuttle, but were rust coloured and hopped like miniature kangaroos. I have yet to discover if the reason that girls no longer jump in my arms is due to the different method of locomotion or more to do with Anno Domini. Far from running away, these mice would sit on their haunches, washing themselves, appearing to watch us with big bush-baby eyes. The colony lived in the calving pens for a couple of years until a black cat took over the family and the farm and mice of any variety faded from the scene. I discovered in retrospect the mice probably were, or rather had been, wood mice. This autumn we picked our usual 28lbs of apples which we stored between layers of newspaper in our new garage. Going to collect a bowl of apples for the house I discovered that three had been eaten right down to the core, the remainder were untouched. I felt, as I set a trap, that this was a poor reward for our visitors' self-discipline, but caught four wood mice before I felt our apple store was reasonably safe. If cats can turn in their grave, our old friend must be known as spinning Sabby whilst her son Sooty sleeps by the fire secure in the knowledge that mouse is a chemical flavour in the 'Choosy' tin.

Two farming friends recently took a well-deserved winter break in Florence. They booked bed and breakfast and ate where the fancy took them. By the end of the week with the lira running low they fancied where they dined much less until on the final evening they had to settle for a decidedly insalubrious cafe. Fortunately, the food tasted better than they had expected. The lady was so impressed with the flan that she asked the waiter for the recipe. He replied in broken English that it was just mice. The husband rose from his chair with his left hand on his stomach and his right holding a handkerchief to his mouth. The waiter wondered if he had made a mistake and retired to consult the chef. He returned and repeated, 'Yes, it was mice'. As the wife rose to join her husband in the rush for the toilet a diner from the next table, with a better grasp of English, leant across to say, 'Yes, it is maize, like in popcorn.'

+++++

One of the animals which, of course, does exercise self-discipline is the squirrel. I recently met one as I drove up Lickpot Hill early on a sunny morning made bright with frost. He was sitting in the road nibbling a titbit collected from his store. As I came upon him his tail bushed out in fright, he dropped his breakfast and ascended the hill appearing to oscillate through the air. The sun reflecting from the frost through his silver tail formed a halo around him. Suddenly, he leaped sideways up the bank on to a hawthorn stump. I stopped to hear what he had to say. He was much too cross to be frightened and although I could not understand the exact words, he told me most eloquently exactly what he thought of imbeciles who drove pick-up trucks on to his breakfast table. The squirrel is a scheduled pest, hated by foresters and gamekeepers but how much brighter the world appears when he is bouncing along the hedgerow beside us.

Perhaps if we could learn his self-discipline we could then enjoy spring instead of spoiling it for everyone else by complaining that we couldn't have another drink for six weeks!

TWELVE

1992

Christmas Eve and twelve of the clock,
'Now they are all on their knees,'
An elder said as we sat in a flock
By the embers in hearthside ease.

We pictured the meek, mild creatures where
They dwelt in their strawy pen,
Nor did it occur to one of us there
To doubt they were kneeling then.

So fair a fancy few would weave
In these years, yet I feel,
If someone said on Christmas Eve,
'Come; see the oxen kneel

In the lonely barton by yonder coomb
Our childhood used to know,'
I should go with him in the gloom,
Hoping it might be so.

Thomas Hardy

Such lovely legends have grown out of the relationship between people and animals particularly where one is dealing with animals on an individual basis. I sometimes feel it is a shame that in this cost-conscious century with mechanical advances enabling one person to care for so many animals, a one to one relationship is less frequently established. No doubt it is because of the joy of establishing this contact that there are more horses in the country today than when they were our prime source of locomotion and power.

When we moved to Milldown, 15 years ago, second son was very upset to learn that we would have no sheep. His uncle solved the problem by sending him a pet lamb. This solution caused as many problems as it solved. Since Ali Ba Ba had no ovine friends, and sheep are essentially flock animals, she decided she was either canine or human and divided her time between Podger, the collie, and the family. Both courses of action had undesirable side effects. Ali's desire to be human led her indoors whenever opportunity arose and ruminants do not housetrain. Keeping her out led to the most heart-rending bleating. When we eventually established a flock, Ali's presence made them impossible to drive. A collie relies almost entirely on bluff and Ali called their bluff, nor did she show any more respect for shepherds. Ultimately, she had to be led back to the farmyard where she spent the rest of her days consuming cattle food in quantities which would have killed any normal sheep. Ali survived, but not her figure, she eventually grew to resemble a barrage balloon on four short legs and became a real problem at shearing time. Of course, we could not part with her, even after she stopped producing one small lamb a year. Years of self-indulgence took their toll and Ali finally quit this mortal coil, leaving her great bulk at the corner of the field closest to the farm. I was relieved that her departure was swift as I had previously been taken severely to task for allowing a sheep to die in a field rather than taking her away for immediate despatch.

I had felt a little hurt over this accusation since we keep our sick and elderly in their home environment as long as possible and severely reprimand those who endeavour to speed their passing. Of course, having animals in our care, whether as pets or for commercial reasons, is a responsibility of which we must all be made aware, but should we create a higher standard for animals than for our own kind?

During the summer we rescued four pea hen eggs from an insecure nest and placed them in the care of a black bantam. Bantams are renowned as good mothers and true to form this one sat, hatched and brooded four pea chicks. Possibly because the climate at Milldown is somewhat more abrasive than the Burmese jungle, we find that pea chicks need to be mollycoddled for much longer than farmyard poultry. The black bantam did not appreciate this. Three months post-hatching and the chicks were as large as the mother and the latter took off to roost in a poplar tree leaving four distraught squeaking babies. Lynda spent several evenings rounding up the unhappy brood before she was relieved of her duties by an unlikely foster parent. One of our surplus Marran cockerels forsook his macho Chanticler image and adopted the orphans. Now, he keeps the family together and finds their food. If other poultry approach they are driven away and at night the youngsters are herded together and led to the safety of a barn. Surplus Marran cockerels are usually fair game for the pot, but I have been told in no uncertain manner that foster dad is strictly off limits.

We have another excellent foster mother on the farm. Fifteen months past, Milldown Teresa had her first calf and showed every sign of becoming a valuable long-term member of the herd. Sadly she was soon struck down by chronic mastitis which rendered her useless for milking. Occasionally, cows will recover from this complaint if they can be persuaded to feed calves for a time. Not all cows are easily convinced that they should feed strange calves. It is instinctive to discipline poachers to protect their own calves' food supply. Fortunately, this instinct was recessive in Teresa's case and she happily fed every calf she was given. At the start of milking we draw back the bolt from the gate of her babies' pen. At the appropriate moment Teresa will open the gate and serve up breakfast or supper. Since she is now fostering her nineteenth and twentieth calf, it is not surprising that she is now known as Mother Teresa.

A lady from Elham has been questioning me about the behaviour of the cattle on Running Hill. They became alarmingly familiar as she walked the footpath through their field. I tried to assure her that they were just showing a friendly interest but was reminded of a family story about Auntie E. Now an octogenarian, Auntie E has long been regarded as the prude of the clan. Apparently, as a teenager she was out for a walk with a mixed bunch of friends and relatives when they ran into a similar problem. In a state of panic, Auntie E stood in the middle of the field and stripped off her dress screaming 'I know it's the red that does it'. Understanding that red is the fashion colour of the year, I look forward to an interesting situation developing.

THIRTEEN

1993

The grass is always greener on the other side of the fence

What are you giving up for Lent? Six weeks without whisky or chocolates may do wonders for the waistline but don't expect much else if the input is purely negative.

Do you remember the advertisement 'Does your dog suffer from hidden hunger?' It assumed that if you did not feed your pet the 'right' brand he was undernourished. There is a saying in farming that 'any bit of wire will hold stock in summer but it takes a good fence in September'. If the grass loses its value animals become restless and search for something better. So don't overdo the fasting bit and be driven to break loose. Nevertheless I had no qualms last October when I turned the bull Beltring Connaught into a field on Lickpot Hill. The grass was lush after the summer soaking and he had twelve nubile heifers for a harem. What more could a healthy Hereford bull desire? I looked at the newly erected fence and thought the taut shining wire would stand any test. Connaught is turned out with heifers every autumn but I had never seen him with as much grass or more securely fenced.

I don't know if it was the extra grass or having less heifers than usual that gave Connaught the impetus to stray. Perhaps some bulls, like some people, are never satisfied. One morning in December second son arrived with the news that Connaught had learnt a new trick. He was threading his horn through the woven wire and lifting the fence so that he could reach underneath with his tongue and graze the verge of the road. Right, I thought, if he's going to spoil the fence he'll have to come in next week. Connaught couldn't wait. The next morning, on her way to work, a worried woman stopped to report that the fence was down and the bull looked like getting out. We investigated and found that twenty yards of fencing was down, the bull was out and gobbling the stolen grass as though suffering from bulimia nervosa.

A passing friend was despatched for reinforcements whilst we stood guard. The escapee suddenly appeared aware that he was under observation, looked acutely embarrassed and scrambled over the flat fence into the field. The fence was re-erected and the stakes driven home 'pdq'. By the time the reinforcements arrived with his chariot, Connaught was contemplatively chewing his cud with his eyes firmly shut as though to keep out the excitement of the morning. He was quickly loaded and returned to his winter quarters where he will spend the next four months on a diet of silage. We hope that by the spring with the grass full of sunshine and sugar and the posts secure in drier soil, Connaught will again respect the discipline of a fence.

Once upon a time, when called upon to recover stray stock, I could put on a pretty fair turn of speed. Over the years my wellingtons appear to have put on weight and now feel like diver's boots if I attempt more than a fast walk, so I have become extremely dependent on the four-legged extensions who accompany me around the farm. When we recently lost our gold collie, Ben, after a series of strokes, I not only lost a faithful friend, but I felt as though I'd lost a leg as well.

Ben was an independent character who did not always conform to the standards expected of a working collie. When sent with the other collies to collect a flock he also found that speed and weight do not go well together and would frequently stop for a roll, but once the sheep were in hand there was none to touch him at penning or disciplining a mutinous ram. Equally fearless with cattle, he had a great sense of humour and never took the job seriously until things got out of hand when he would effortlessly take control and solve the problem. He was the sergeant major of our unit, rigorously disciplining the other dogs and loved by the children as a trustworthy live cuddly toy. As a friend he is irreplaceable and for work we hope to train one of his seven grandchildren who arrived at Christmas. Lynda tells me I have to practise self-discipline long past Lent as training a puppy needs a lot of patience.

FOURTEEN

1993

The badger grunting on his woodland track
With shaggy hide and sharp nose scrowed with black
Roots in the bushes and the woods and makes
A great huge burrow in the ferns and brakes
With nose on ground he runs an awkward pace
And anything will beat him in the race.

John Clare

Sometime past the wife of a farming relative told me she had been woken early one summer morning by a fracas in the henhouse. She had projected her slumbering spouse from the bed with one swift kick and aimed him at the door, shouting, 'Fox!'. Before he had regained consciousness he was walking into the dawn clad as God had created him, except for a double-barrelled twelve bore. Suddenly becoming aware of the propriety of the situation, he grabbed his hat and jammed it on his head before stalking barefoot through the wet grass to raise the siege. The fox made good his escape, leaving behind a headless cockerel, although it is rumoured that shortly afterwards he died of laughter.

Many years ago, an uncle told me he had had a disaster with his point-of-lay pullets. In those days it was standard practice for all farmers' wives to keep twenty or thirty hens to provide them with pin money. Just before Christmas my uncle had been woken by loud cackling and suspected poultry thieves. When he arrived at the poultry shed a door was hanging on one hinge and in the light of the moon he saw a badger chasing the twenty-five pullets round the shed. In a panic he fired both barrels at the intruder who shot out between his legs bowling him over and disappeared into the night. A count revealed eleven dead birds most of which had died of gunshot wounds than by tooth and claw. All this happened many years ago and, being rather green at the time, I was somewhat surprised as I had been brought up to believe that foxes lived off chicken and badgers ate worms and beetles.

Having lived longer, I now realise that a sow badger will eat just about anything she can get her jaws round. I have no evidence either way on the boar badger but most of the attacks I am aware of have been at the time of year when the sows are carrying or feeding cubs. Now that we live in more civilised times, protecting ones stock is more tricky. Taking a gun in pursuit of poultry thieves is not permitted, much less shooting a badger. A farmer who peacefully persuaded some badgers to move to a less inconvenient spot was recently punished more severely than a student who raped another student, a woman who murdered her husband or a car thief who ran down two children.

Being all too aware of the priorities with which society maintains the law, I was put on the spot when Lynda told me that a hen and chicks had been taken from a coop. The claw marks on the woodwork and the pile of feathers was conclusive evidence of a badger attack. Not wishing to spend my declining years rotting on Dartmoor, I banished all ideas of reprisals from my mind. However, I could not leave the remaining hens and chicks unprotected so I erected an electric fence around the remaining arks. This would give a short sharp message to an intruder to seek supper elsewhere without causing her any harm.

Two nights later I arrived home from a meeting to find Lynda waiting for me by the door. A neighbour had phoned from a mile away to ask if we still had Podger, our 16 year-old Collie. A dog like him was running around the lanes apparently lost. As a jaunty two year-old, with a nose for the lasses, it was not unknown for Podger to wander, but 14 long years and one short operation later sans eyes, sans taste, sans everything, he is allowed the freedom of the farm and never strays. A short inspection showed a Podgerless farm and an electric fence in a terrific tangle. Evidently he had wandered into the protected area and, not seeing the wire, become disorientated and terrified before taking off in a blind panic, or had we discovered the secret of eternal youth? Podger didn't think so when we found him completely lost a mile from home. Now Podger is shut in before the fence goes on at night and so far the rest of the poultry have survived.

The other evening, I followed a badger up Lickpot Hill. It trotted in my lights with the gait of a seaman who has spliced the main-brace once too often, the fluffy grey bottom rolling from side to side. It was in no hurry to leave the road - why should it be? The family had probably followed that same trail before our ancestors walked over from Europe.

I still believe that the vast majority of badgers live off grubs, beetles and carrion. I see ample proof of this each day as I walk the fields and lanes. Proof also that there are more badgers about than at any time over the last fifty years. I do hope that an increase in numbers of the two dominant species in the area does not lead to a clash which could only lead to one disastrous result. If it does it will have been brought forward by a bureaucracy creating blanket laws to solve a problem which is specific to the countryside. Are not we all suffering from having our lives run by specialists, those experts who know more and more about less and less until they know everything about nothing?

FIFTEEN

1993

One boy's a boy, two boys is half a boy and
three boys is no B. Boy at all.

Flora Thompson

Probably not the mathematics taught in the National Curriculum, but nevertheless an adage which I have found very true when training puppies. Two months after Lyndsey's happy event four puppies were placed in new homes. Lass was booked to leave a month later when her new owners had finished lambing. This would leave us with Jet, who we planned to keep, and Little Nell. At first, three two month-old puppies seemed less than seven, but within a fortnight there appeared to be seventy times seven. To shut them in their shed I needed a nimble assistant, a large bowl of food and a fair slice of luck. When walking them one would decide to return to check there were no second helpings, just as the other two thought there might be a cat having a peaceful nap the other side of Barham. It was with considerable relief that we handed Lass over to her new owners to learn the task of a sheep and cattle dog. By now Jet and Nell were increasing in size, speed, appetite and the ability to wreak havoc over the whole farm. Left for two minutes they would set off to search for fresh mischief. Then they discovered the midden. Puppies rapidly lose their cuddly appeal when they have spent the last ten minutes burying each other in six months' scrapings from the cattle yard.

Then the telephone rang. 'Yes we have one bitch pup available. Yes he could call in half an hour.' Thirty minutes of washing and brushing rendered Nell reasonably presentable. I can hardly ever see an animal leave the farm without some feeling of regret. This time it was coated with a double helping of relief. Jet had no such mixed feelings. He took a while to realise that his playmate was not returning and then seemed to lose all zest for life. When released from his shed he would search for Nell and then return to the darkest corner of his sanctuary. Three days later he started digging a large hole in the spot where Nell had accumulated her trophies, the boots, shoes, cat dishes and keys which she had filched. It seemed he was burying her memory and his puppyhood. From then on he has followed us and his father and mother, bright and cheerful, but no longer an irresponsible and uncontrollable puppy. Now he is learning to keep to heel because he wants to be with us. He is learning his job by filling in his spare time by playing with the adult collies their favourite game of moving ducks and chickens round the farm.

Jet cannot help with the sheep for they are too aggressive while the lambs are small. He would probably receive a beating which could put him off work for life. We usually move sheep from pen to pen by carrying the lamb just off the ground so the ewe will follow. Today the ewe I was moving was so incensed at my intrusion into the family circle that she launched a really vicious attack. I was completely outgunned and had to release the lamb much to the amusement of Lynda and senior son. Without their lambs they are still, timid, helpless creatures as individuals, but in a flock, when motivated by greed and envy, they have an almost human ability to become a mob. Feeding a flock of a hundred or so ewes requires all the guile and resourcefulness I can muster. I approach the field from different directions and make dummy runs to create confusion, but still lose control at times even with the help of Lyndsey and Smartie. One does not feel dignified riding backwards round a field on a large sheep pursued by her 99 demented colleagues, and yet I know that any of these animals on their own would retreat from a cat or my smallest grandson.

SIXTEEN

1993

The sleep-flower sways in the wheat its head,
Heavy with dreams as that with bread:
The goodly grain and the sun-flushed sleeper
The reaper reaps, and Time the reaper.
I hang 'mid men my needless head,
And my fruit is dreams, as theirs is bread:
The goodly men and the sun-hazed sleeper
Time shall reap, but after the reaper
The world shall glean of me, me the sleeper.

Francis Thompson

There have been times when Milldown has been in danger of being overrun by poultry of all shapes and sizes. It is not that we breed them but nature, 'I am told' abhors a vacuum and, it appears, an uninhabited pile of bales. Ignore a haystack for a month and a proud bantam will emerge with a mixed batch of chicks, ducks and odd guinea fowl. About the only object they fail to incubate is the occasional golf ball I have slipped in to check this profusion. No doubt many fall prey to a foraging fox or badger whilst others learn too late why the chicken failed to cross the road, but this is the price of freedom. For every one we lost there were two to take its place. This spring we suddenly realised that our chicken numbers were becoming sadly depleted and not a duck remained. I phoned the 'lone ranger' who helps us preserve the law in these situations. He arrived to meet a vixen leaving the barn with her latest victim. The problem, which we had anticipated would take nights of patient vigil, was solved with one shot. After weeks of easy pickings our villain had become over-confident.

A few mornings later I met another overconfident fox. Driving home from Newchurch in the middle of the morning I saw him at the side of the lane tearing a refuse liner to pieces. I passed slowly within six feet of him. Whatever the bag contained it proved of more interest than a passing motorist. Perhaps he felt that a useful scavenger deserved to remain unmolested, which he was. Two more young foxes have been observing me over the past month. Their mother had taken over part of an old badger sett. Perhaps she was aware of the draconian laws protecting these earthworks and felt she could cash in on this legal defence.

One or two cubs regularly watched me driving round and working with the sheep. I had lost no lambs to them and was content to remain the subject of their scrutiny. They had had no experience to teach them that I was their natural enemy and instinctive caution was outweighed by youthful curiosity.

Another young predator who learnt that experience can be a very costly method of acquiring knowledge was a magpie. It was hopping in the road as I drove to and from the field with loads of silage. Eventually, I noticed he had been run over. The parent birds were scavenging the other side of the hedge. It occurred to me that any other corpse lying in that road would immediately become dinner for these inveterate pirates who will readily devour the eyes of a mislaid ewe before death has relieved her need of them. All day long the magpies searched for slugs and snails without turning their attention to the body in the road. A few days later I witnessed the same occurrence with a pair of crows. Perhaps even corvids have some finer feelings or is it that their flesh is too rank for even their catholic taste?

Stepping over a hurdle whilst checking the cattle at Paddlesworth, I saw a squirrel on the grass about twenty yards from me. Although he was facing me his attention was riveted on a peacock which stood between us. I froze and remained the statue of Eros as the little drama unfolded. The squirrel wanted to walk along the edge of the field past the peacock to a sheltering oak. Every time he moved forward his tormentor stretched his neck closing the gap between his beak and the fence. The little animal could have made a detour but he would have placed himself at a disadvantage by moving into open country and I believe, more importantly, he would have lost face in giving trail to a mere bird, albeit a bird ten times his size. Three times he sallied forward but was turned back by the threatening beak to sit on his haunches chattering his disapproval. The fourth time pride overcame fear and he rushed past his elephantine opponent then turned, almost on my boot, to express his contempt for all things feathered. He then hopped past me in no great hurry until I turned to observe. Discretion proved the better part of valour as in a flash he disappeared up the oak.

Many people told me last summer how much they enjoyed the vivid scarlet display of poppies at Milldown. Their appreciation was about the only thing I did receive. The beans, which I had planted, were almost completely smothered by the 'devil's flower'. Weeds, or the art of growing the wrong plant in the wrong place at the wrong time, are proving to be the greatest hazard in my experiment with organic farming. This year, forewarned and forearmed, the oats, which follow the beans, have been harrowed heavily three times. After each harrowing they appeared to have suffered more severely but I hope that those of you who are waiting for the hills to be painted red will be sadly disappointed. The oats are now recovering from their mistreatment. Cereals may not be human, but, like us, their lives often become choked with problems and trivia. It can be a harrowing experience facing these impediments but unless we do we cannot expect to emerge strong and healthy as the oats but be smothered and overcome as were the beans.

SEVENTEEN

1993

Give me juicy autumnal fruit ripe and red from the orchard,
Give me a field where the unmowed grass grows,
Give me an arbour, give me the trellised grape,
Give me fresh corn and wheat,
give me serene-moving animals teaching content.

Walt Whitman

What a discontented species we are. 45 years ago, with my soft fingers burning from the onslaught of thistle-laden sheaves, I would daydream of miraculous cures for weeds which did not involve my aching back when hoeing, and of wheat fields which would all yield the biblical one hundred-fold. Since then, chemicals have been developed which are capable of sending the thistles back to Scotland

and producing crops of wheat near the hundred-fold. So, am I now sitting back with cool fingers enjoying the cornucopia which science has offered? Not me, I'm running around in ever decreasing circles attempting to remember the old techniques of producing a 40-fold crop without modern aids and hoping the combine doesn't block up cutting a patch of thistles.

Of course, I can summon many arguments to justify my perverse behaviour. If we continue to increase the use of finite resources at the present rate we shall rapidly reach the day of reckoning and face famine of an unprecedented scale. No one can know for certain the long-term effects of the chemicals we use, perhaps we are poisoning the planet. I am certain that crops which are not forced to maximum yield produce food which is more tasty and possibly more nutritious. The politicians and the press persuade us that we are producing too much food so perhaps by reducing my yields I am performing a public service.

The case is quite convincing to a well-fed member of the western society with a long life expectancy who is concerned for the state of the planet in seventy years' time. It is undoubtedly less so to the African mother whose child will die in seven days if food aid does not arrive. It is probably true that feeding the child will add to the increase in world population, which is arguably the greatest threat to our existence, but there can be no moral argument for infanticide by starvation. At present, most starvation is caused by problems of economics and distribution. I find that my best organic production is about two thirds of that produced using chemicals so if society were to reject the use of chemicals entirely, we should face wholesale famine through lack of food. What price then on nitrogen levels in the water?

+++++

Earlier this year it was my privilege to meet a lady who had been born at Milldown in the early part of the century. She was the youngest of eight children. Her father was the local 'skin man'. He made his living collecting up animals which had died, skinning them and, when he had a cart load, selling them to the tannery in Canterbury. Milldown, which is seldom without a stiff breeze, was the ideal spot for the trade.

Even in those more tolerant times the skin man would not have been a popular neighbour. He also farmed about fifty acres. Without the aid of chemical fertiliser the light sandy soil did little more than provide the family and horse with subsistence. What is now one of my most fertile fields was known as Brakey as it only grew bracken which provided bedding for the horse and cattle in the winter. The only fuel for heating and cooking was wood which the younger children had to gather from the hedgerows. The youngest daughter remembers the kitchen range as a dragon with an insatiable appetite.

On a hot summer day in 1914 the father set off to Canterbury with a load of skins. The four eldest children accompanied him to hold back the cart to avoid overloading the horse down the steep hill. Mother took the younger children to the hayfield to collect any wood from the outside before the hay was mown. When a terrific storm broke they ran for home dragging what wood they could manage. As the mother opened the door, the kitchen burst into flames for the house had been struck by lightning. She then had to leave the four small children and run a mile to the nearest 'phone, so it is not surprising that by the time the horse drawn fire engine arrived from Bridge the house was well ablaze The only water on site was the underground tank collecting rain for domestic use. The firemen refused to use this realising that the family could not exist without water, so ran out pipes to a pond a quarter of a mile distant only to discover that it was empty. The firemen could only stand and comfort the family as the house burnt to the ground. There were no social services to help the homeless, but although times were difficult, or perhaps because of this, there was a strong sense of community and all the family were accommodated until the landlord rebuilt the house. Two of the elder boys lodged with Mr Wilcox who had recently become headmaster of Elham School. The family continued to farm at Milldown until 1944. Then the War Agriculture Committee insisted that part of the farm should be ploughed to produce more wheat and the elderly farmer retired as he had no arable equipment and no money to buy any.

Now the EEC is insisting that I produce less cereals so the wheel has turned full circle. Like most of my generation I have periods of nostalgia for the good old days and I shall continue to experiment with organic farming so long as it is economically viable. I am thankful that I did not have to cope with farming seventy years ago. I am even more thankful that I do not have to answer the moral question, which way should governments, and indirectly the electorate, decide that agriculture should proceed. It is more than enough to me to plan my own little patch.

EIGHTEEN

1994

Behold a giant am I!
Aloft here in my tower.
With my granite jaws I devour
The maize, and the wheat, and the rye,
And grind them in to flour.
I look down over the farms;
In the field of grain I see
The harvest that is to be.
And I fling to the air my arms.
For I know it is all for me.
I stand here in my place.
With my foot on the rock below.
And whichever way it may blow I meet it face to face.
As a brave man meets his foe.

HW Longfellow

When I was a small boy, walking round the stock with my father, one of my great pleasures was to drink from the little streams which erupted from the foot of the downs. This was the water of life, rising in the spring to bring life to creation. It certainly tasted better than its cousin which gushed from a tap, whether because it defied the ban on drinking stream water or because it had not been treated with chlorine I don't know. More and more it is dictated to us what we can drink, how our food must be treated, how long we can work, what we must say that I begin to feel that I am a battery bird. If I were, I would probably feel safer than our very free-range poultry at the moment. Three times in one week we have had a daylight visit from a very self-confident fox. On Monday I was watching my son ploughing until he was moved on by Bella, the Alsatian. On Tuesday in poor early morning light I thought Jet, the Collie, had jumped the gun when I saw a sleek dark form apparently rounding up the sheep, and on Wednesday he was sitting in the road by the milking parlour watching my daughter-in-law milking.

A few evenings later our solitary Muscovy duck was missing. I vowed vengeance on our visitor. The odd chicken might be poached with impunity, it is difficult to establish a one to one relationship with a chicken, but ducks are different. I remembered the first individual duck we had reared. Lynda had set a few duck eggs under a bantam. When they did not burst from their shells on the appointed day, she impatiently broke them open to find that one contained a live duckling. Overcome with remorse she wrapped the cracked egg in a flannel and hid it in the airing cupboard. A few days later a wet yellow duckling emerged. Our three children were quite small at the time and made a great pet of her. When she grew up she slept under our oil tank and, after laying her daily egg, would march to the garden and quack impatiently for Lynda to come and dig for worms. Never before or since has our garden been so well dug. One day our daughter came in crying, the boys had stolen her doll's pram. It seemed fairly unlikely that two boys, aged nine and seven, would be seen walking through the village with a pram but Theresa was inconsolable so we investigated. The pram had indeed been requisitioned as a suitable conveyance for Dilly. They had taken her for about half a mile to the village stream for a swimming lesson. By the time we arrived on the scene the coaching had obviously been a great success and Dilly was having the time of her life. One morning she was not waiting for worms and no amount of searching produced a clue to her whereabouts. A rumour circulated that she had been ducknapped by envious children from the town. Two or four legged predators, we will never know, but the garden quickly reverted to nature. This time the Muscovy was more fortunate and the following night was back in her shed.

I have been on fairly intimate terms with a number of animals of a variety of species but none of them has ever confided to me the secret of whether they prefer freedom or security. I know that on a sunny day in spring cattle, who have been yarded all winter, will shoot through the gate at the first opportunity and bolt for fresh green grass. It is a very different picture when I try to drive the same cattle to the freedom of the fields through an autumnal squall.

Hurrying through Ashford street market in the rain I spotted a damp and dispirited trader selling off his garden ornaments at half price. A little windmill with rotating sweeps seemed ideal for our patio so it was swiftly purchased and installed overlooking the valley as its giant predecessor had for over three hundred years. Coincidentally, it had last been worked in 1916 by James May, a distant relative of Lynda's. My grandfather was also a miller at Cheriton, relying on wind power until 1902 when the sweeps broke off and landed on the dog kennel. Fortunately, Ben, the much-loved family retriever, escaped unharmed but the mill was then converted to gas. Even with this double connection it is difficult to believe that an attraction for windmills can be transmitted through the genes but our little mill has a strange hold over Daniel, our youngest grandson. Dan is a free spirit quite prepared to take life on the chin but, although he will not allow a visit to pass without watching the windmill, he insists on an escort and keeps a respectful distance.

Grandad also finds few sights more evocative than rotating sweeps. To me it is miraculous to see the beneficial and mighty power generated by harnessing the malign and invisible force of the wind. Even more the sight tells the story of our ancestors. It tells of a community which revolved around the mill, of farmers who brought their corn to the local miller for grinding into flour for the local baker who provided bread for the village; provided bread for John Hogben, the Lyminge carpenter, who repaired the sweeps when, in 1891, a sudden change in wind direction caught the miller off guard and part of the sweeps landed in Wick Farm, Acrise. They tell us the story of a village independent and interdependent. Just as for hundreds of years those slowly revolving arms reminded our ancestors of the wheel of life, showed them each Easter how life is followed by death, and death by resurrection as they 'lifted their eyes unto the hills'.

NINETEEN

1994

The wolf will live with the lamb … and a little child shall lead them.

Isaiah 11.6.

I recently took a morning off from the chores of the lambing shed to attend a farm dispersal sale. Few of us can resist this chance of picking up a valuable machine at a bargain price although, with dozens of dealers and hundreds of hopeful farmers in attendance, the genuine bargains are few and far between. But if one is not an optimist one wouldn't be a farmer and there are few better opportunities for superannuated agricultural students to hold a reunion, for picking up the country gossip or finding a sympathetic ear to listen to complaints about the Ministry of Agriculture, or the weather. A dispersal is also an excellent opportunity for rewarding a 'Farmer's Wife' with a day off. Of course, the wife of a farmer who might just as easily have been the partner of a plumber, priest or professor, could be easily satisfied with a day in Oxford Street followed by a night on the town or perhaps a couple of weeks on the Riviera.

Those of us in the trade who are responsible for a genuine 'FW' realise that she is a particularly delicate person with specific needs which are in constant need of attention. The species cannot survive without having its feet immersed in six inches of mud at no more than eight hourly intervals. Serious damage can occur if its programme of producing at least three hot meals a day is interrupted except by the celebration of cleaning human and canine footprints off the kitchen floor. An excess of energy, leading to a dangerous condition known as a 'shopping spree' can only be averted by providing at least a ton of bales to be moved daily. Withdrawal symptoms are likely to occur if a young weakly animal does not need to be coaxed back to life at least once every twelve hours or delinquent cattle need to be driven back to the safety of their yards by moonlight. At a sale, members of the species congregate together around items which have already been sold to avoid the auctioneer's banter interrupting the vital passage of information as to who is begetting whom. This arrangement is approved by the said auctioneers as it prevents the 'FW's from stopping their respective spouses from vying with one another to spend more than they can afford on particularly useless items of machinery. The inconvenience of not leaving an 'FW' at home to attend to such tasks as need attention can be partly offset against the convenience of having someone to settle the account whilst one listens to the tale of why lambs resembling Fred's tup appeared in six adjoining parishes, collect coffee and hot dogs, load five lots of junk into the truck and help push out a mate who was fool enough to bring a two wheel drive car. Thus a good time is had by all.

On this occasion I acquired a fertiliser spinner. The following morning second son was despatched on a tractor to collect my bargain from the Faversham area. I remembered the tale of Harry, my father's one-time waggoner. His previous employer had purchased a shire gelding from the brewery at Faversham. When Harry was told that tomorrow he was to walk from Newington to Faversham, a round trip of fifty miles to a town he had never visited and collect the horse, he commented 'I'd better bring a bit of dinner, then'. 'Dinner?' came the reply, 'if you get up in the morning you'll be back by dinner-time'. Times change for if second son had been told to walk to Faversham and back in a morning his reply would have been unprintable. If he had undertaken the journey he would have needed a second shire to carry his supplies and the guarantee of a barrel of their best bitter on the brewery horse. On a hundred horse-power tractor he arrived back by noon without suffering severe malnutrition.

Who can predict what style of life will be expected by the time my youngest grandson has grown up. At two and a half he is finding his first lambing a magic experience to be savoured to the full. He does become alarmed if he believes a lamb is coming to harm. The first problem birth he viewed I was holding the ewe whilst Lynda had ropes attached to the front legs round her shoulders so as to use her full weight in pulling. I have known fully-experienced cow persons blanch at the force needed to produce something as small and apparently delicate as a lamb. In this case Dan was obviously distressed and stomped up and down the feeding passage disclaiming 'No, no, Nanny, don't pull its legs off'. If a ewe loses a lamb we sometimes resort to the time-honoured practice of skinning the dead lamb and fitting the skin like a jacket to an orphan or rejected lamb. This usually convinces the ewe that her baby has been resuscitated. The nose usually reminds us when it is time to remove the outer skin. When Dan came upon Lynda removing such a skin he refused to accept her assurances that she was not harming the lamb and hurriedly left her as she ignored his protests. After completing her smelly task, Lynda sought out her grandson to comfort him but he had already found consolation. He was sitting in the corner of a straw pen, his right thumb in his mouth, his left arm round an orphan lamb with Smartie, the collie's head laid protectively upon his lap as contentment and sleep crept over him. We should not be surprised at the season of Pentecost that communications can cross the barriers of language and species.

TWENTY

1994

His lambs outnumber a noon's roses,
Yet when night's shadows fall,
His blind old sheep dog, Slumber-soon,
Misses not one of all.
His are the quiet steeps of dreamland,
The waters of no-more-pain;
His ram's bell rings 'neath an arch of stars,
'Rest, rest and rest again'

Walter de la Mare

Three days of sunshine, of rushing and hard work and shearing was over for another year. The hard work is done by a contractor but Lynda is kept busy rolling the fleeces whilst I play chess, with sheep as pieces, trying to ensure that there is a constant supply for the shearer and that the various groups are not mixed up. Last year the wool market collapsed. When we received our wool cheque there was just sufficient to cover the cost of shearing. This year the trade has improved, but there is no prospect of us seeing again viable sheep farming for wool production in this country. It is a far cry from some three hundred years ago when villages were razed to the ground to make way for 'the golden hoof' and the large red wool-filled cushion, the woolsack, was established as the seat of the Lord Chancellor to remind the Lords whereon the wealth of the country was based.

Still, the fleece must be removed. A soiled or damp fleece provides an ideal resting site for the common blowfly and a sheep an ideal larder for their larvae. 'All flesh is grass' but there must be less painful means of meeting the end than to be eaten alive by maggots. To the ancient Hebrews sheep were a form of currency and a man's wealth was measured by the size of his flock. Wolves and bears were the equivalent of the modern bank robber. I don't imagine that the bank clerks at Lyminge would be too impressed if I turned up with a truck load of lambs to settle my account charges. Today the only economic reason for keeping sheep is for the meat market. Without this there would be no return to cover the millions of pounds spent every year on fencing fields, feeding flocks and tending them in sickness. The countryside would change as more and more lowland was ploughed and the hills were given over to rabbits and ramblers. Millions of lambs would lose the chance of enjoying a summer freely grazing and the breeding flocks would be slaughtered. The sheep which once made Britain great would become extinct except for a few in rare breed centres. Is it not strange that the biggest threat today comes not from wolves and bears but from maggots and vegetarians?

I don't suppose that a lamb grazing in a meadow ponders how its carcase will be disposed of after its demise, such imaginings are left to humankind. A grand old lady of my acquaintance willed that her body should be cut up and fed to her beagle pack. This caused considerable controversy and I fear her wishes were not carried out. It does not seem strange to me that one who had cared for her sheep and hounds for so many years, should prefer to gallop with them over the hills she loved, rather than be left to moulder 'Beneath those rugged elms that yew trees shade'.

It is not usually my task to milk the cows but when my son and daughter-in-law took a holiday I was taken off the shelf, dusted and told to get on with it. To update myself I did a milking with my daughter-in-law. The first cow in was Sandra, the best cow we have ever bred and as such a somewhat pampered prima donna. She has learnt to tap the feed delivery spout with her head and keep a constant supply of nuts rolling into her manger. Because of her extraordinary ability as a milk producer, and the fact that whatever she eats is returned threefold in milk, this behaviour is accepted. After a batch of cows has been milked a gate lifts and they walk out. I turned the switch, the gate lifted, Sandra tapped out her code for more nuts. I shouted for her to walk out. She looked at me disdainfully and tapped for still more nuts. Lucy drew my attention to a short length of plastic water pipe and told me to lift it in the air. Although well out of reach it was sufficient to remind Sandra that even prima donnas can overstep the mark and she walked out like a normal cow. It was sufficient to remind me that for the next fortnight I wasn't just milking a herd but caring for 80 individual cows.

TWENTY-ONE

1994

One for sorrow, two for joy,
Three for a girl, four for a boy,
Five for silver, six for gold,
Seven for a secret never to be told.

Traditional

We have all been moved by the heroic efforts of the Webb family to relieve some of the suffering in Romania in such a practical way. Lacking their energy and initiative my attention was caught by an advertisement in a farming magazine asking for farm machinery to equip a one hundred acre farm in that country. They were not looking for the multi thousand pound state of the art machines on display at the Smithfield Show, but rather the simple, easy to maintain, tools which we used fifty years ago. Scanning the list I noted the need for a drill to sow maize and sugar beet. I remembered that Lynda's mother had one buried in a barn at Paddlesworth. She readily agreed to give this to the cause.

All I had to do to assuage my conscience was to dig it out, check that it was still in working order and deliver it to Alfriston for shipment. I commandeered a stalwart assistant and started stage one. An hour later, and about a ton of guano to the good, one would hardly know that the drill had spent the last fifteen years as a peacock perch. Another hour spent moving more recently abandoned pieces of potato equipment and we had cleared a track to the door where we could mount it on a tractor. We each took one side. 'Right', I commanded, 'When I say lift, lift'. The left side assailed by fourteen stone of youthful muscle, inched forward, my side remained rooted to the spot. 'I think this side's stuck', I called. We changed ends. The right side moved forward. Eventually my exhausted assistant and the drill reached the door. A check in daylight revealed that this machine had two barrels for sowing different sizes of seed. My father-in-law had never grown maize so the most vital option was missing. I was pleasantly surprised at the enthusiastic co-operation I received from local agricultural engineers who discovered the manufacturers of the drill still making farm machines in Scotland. Unfortunately, they did not still make drills and had no idea from where to obtain a barrel.

Weeks slipped into months and the essential equipment could not be located and then, within a fortnight of D-day, the farming grapevine came to my rescue. A cousin told me that an ex-neighbour at Newington had a Russel Root Drill. He only used the two smaller barrels and Romania was welcome to the maize barrel. How often do we seek far and wide for the answer that lies at hand? All we had to do now was load the machine sideways into my livestock box and transport it to Sussex. An hour later with a gear box and wheel still protruding from the box I realised that I would need a battalion of marines to assist with the unloading. Plan B was to scrounge a pukka low load trailer. Once again a friendly machinery dealer came to my rescue, the drill was lifted on to the trailer with the farm loader all ready for the fifty mile trip to Sussex. Wheels are not the most easily secured objects and after five miles I had stopped five times until ropes and nerves were at maximum tension. Thereafter it was downhill all the way with two brothers waiting to unload me with a farm loader. A motley collection of items was assembled awaiting a forty-foot trailer which the post office was supplying for transport. When I recalled all the people who had made a contribution to my one small item, I realised what a tremendous amount of unseasonal Christmas spirit and goodwill was contained in this lorry load.

TWENTY-TWO

1995

From troubles of the world,
I turn to ducks.
Beautiful, comical things.

FW Harvey

Walk through any supermarket at the moment and one would be forgiven for thinking that Easter is the feast of eggs. I suppose there is a certain symbolism in an apparently lifeless egg bursting forth with new life, especially when the new creation is a duckling, hatched with a smile on its face, the picture of perfect innocence, the little friend of the world. Of course, many of these soft downy creatures grow into drakes which do have a darker side.

Soon after we moved to Milldown a friend offered us three Muscovy ducks 'or perhaps two ducks and a drake'. Acquaintances in Wales had a pair which kept their table liberally supplied with tender meaty fowl, so, accepting the offer seemed a good idea at the time. A little more time proved we had become the proud owners of three Muscovy drakes. Whilst the female of the species is a fairly versatile creature, laying eggs, sitting on and hatching them, protecting the helpless young and rearing them, the male has but one purpose and aim in life. In the absence of any ducks this aim is rigorously pursued with any feathered object from a passing sparrow to a feathered cushion which a litter lout has left by the roadside. It was imperative that we introduced feminine interest to our Muscovy flock. Lynda's aunt presented us with a gentle, friendly duck named Alice. For three days, she delighted us by laying an egg a day until, overcome by the ardour of her suitors, she ended it all under the wheels of a passing lorry. At this stage, fate, in a red coat and a bushy tail, stepped in and removed the smallest drake. Three nights later he returned for Big Billy Drake Gruff. We found our champion in the morning tattered but triumphant on a pile of white feathers and red hair.

I don't know what became of our visitor, he had obviously learnt, as I did much later, that a mature Muscovy drake, if not immortal, is virtually indestructible. I give little credence to rumours of sightings of a fox in the mist of dawn grazing clover and nibbling mushrooms, although Isaiah predicts such unlikely events. We eventually obtained two concubines for our remaining drakes. We carefully saved the eggs and when the ducks went broody sat them each on thirteen eggs in secure arks. After 32 days we checked for any signs of hatching and discovered only 14 eggs remained. We had a rat with a penchant for omelette. Lynda lost patience, declared the eggs were infertile and broke one open to prove it. It wasn't. Eventually nine ducklings emerged. We returned home one sunny morning to find two crows had developed a taste for duckling. One would make a mock attack and allow itself to be driven off by two frantic mothers whilst its partner would attack from the rear and carry off another duckling. We shut up the two ducks with the remaining five babies.

Friends arrived one evening and admired the statues by the door. They thought they almost looked real, which was not surprising as our two drakes had so exhausted themselves by their efforts that they appeared to have turned to stone. Later that evening, we were disturbed by the flapping of wings. We found the mothers impotently stamping and hissing whilst a hedgehog gobbled up its third course. Duckling are either terribly brave or extremely stupid, smiling constantly at a world bent on their immediate destruction.

+++++

The next time round, the ducks decided to do without our assistance, they laid their eggs in a completely inaccessible nest under our chicken house and emerged five weeks later with twenty-two offspring. Most of these survived. Although the parent birds are too heavy to gain lift off the young ones all think they should learn to fly. They half climbed, half flew, to the top of the workshop roof. As more reached their vantage point and pushed to the front, the early arrivals were forced to make a lemming-like power dive to the ground. As they gained in confidence and experience they attained two or three circuits of the farm before landing. To walk across the yard in the morning with three pound ducks skimming at head height out of the sun and out of control, required nerves of steel and a strong umbrella. It was time for the surplus drakes to add variety to the family table.

+++++

Farming is no career for the squeamish and I have been called on various occasions to save sheep further suffering with a humane killer, to use a shot gun to send cats involved in road accidents to a better place or with a quick flick of the wrist to practise euthanasia on aged chickens. Muscovy drakes are a problem. They won't hold their heads still for a humane killer, a shot gun is not an option for taking one bird out of a flock and a quick flick of the wrist produced a blink of one eye which said 'you'll have to do better than that'.

At last I devised a scheme which would be instantaneous and infallible. I summoned the assistance of my two sons, then aged 12 and 14. Senior son was to stand in a water tank and hold the drake. Second son stood outside the tank and steadied the victim's head. With one blow of a pick axe handle I would decapitate the bird which would not even know what was happening. Senior son was always the squeamish member of the family. At the critical moment he pulled away from his task as executioner's assistant which dragged second son's thumb across the edge of the water tank. The drake died instantly. I was a little surprised at the range of a 12 year old's vocabulary but I gathered that the rest of the drakes could die of old age.

For the past 15 years Lynda and I have had to drive the ducks to bed every night. They perform no economic function but if they stay out a fox might come and kill the ducks and we should be left with just the drakes and the whole performance would have to be repeated. Sometimes it is easier just to admit defeat.

TWENTY-THREE
1995

House mate I can think you still
Bounding to the window-sill,
Over which I vaguely see
Your small mound beneath the tree
Showing in the autumn shade
That you moulder where you played.

Thomas Hardy

Long before the previous owner of Milldown had considered selling up, I moved in with my family and illicitly harvested our first crop. My defence is that I did not know the copse of chestnut was part of the farm. Of course, I, of all people, know that everywhere belongs severally or separately to someone but, believing that someone to be the Ministry of Defence, I used this as an excuse to take my wife and three primary school age children scrumping chestnuts. Of course, such an exercise could not be accomplished stealthily with such a crew. The three junior poachers were seized by the farmer believing them to be vandals wrecking his beehives. He could have been excused for thinking ten boat loads of Vikings had returned to sack the Elham Valley. When the adult members surrendered and apologised for our error, the hostages were released and he declined our offer to surrender our booty.

Surely it is a call from our primeval past that a middle-aged farmer is prepared to tear his fingers to shreds and be made to look a complete fool to collect a few nuts which he could well afford to buy from the supermarket. What a wonderful autumn this has been for the hunter gatherer. Of course, we eat and enjoy cultivated mushrooms for 11 months of the year, but they cannot hold a candle to the wild ones picked with the dew on them and flavoured with 'for free' sauce. Two thousand years on it is still a joy to reap where one has not sown and gather where one has not strayed. Blackberries have burgeoned from the bushes and sloes squealed to be submerged in gin, cherry plums rained on our heads as my grandson, Daniel, and I scooped them into buckets. Of all the hedgerow harvest our favourite is the scad. A little closer to a small sour damson than a large sweet sloe, even ripe it will set the teeth on edge when eaten raw, but what flavour it adds to pies and crumbles. The family never tire of the jam and gallons of the fruit go in to a rich full-flavoured wine. They have two drawbacks, a lot of stones and a name which some find unpleasantly unappetising. Second son set out on a quest to discover an alternative title. Those who know his name will appreciate his delight when in an old book of hedgerow plants he found them referred to as 'Kirk's Blue Plums'. This he considers gives him first claim to most of the jam and all of the wine.

+++++

I was brought up with cats on the farm and humans in the house and for many years resisted my children's pleas for a pet cat. We returned home one Saturday afternoon to find a very small, very pregnant, very hungry black cat in the calf pens. I eventually succumbed to my daughter's pleading - on condition it stays outside and works for a living. Black Sabbath or Sabby as she soon became known, must have heard my ultimatum for she set about removing the, very considerable, plague of mice in a manner I would never have thought possible. Eventually, the only mice remaining on the farm were those which had taken refuge in the house to escape the black death, whereupon I had no option but to allow Sabby inside to complete her task. She would have been a perfectly satisfactory house cat if it wasn't for her penchant for chicken. On one occasion she started clawing my leg, as soon as a roast fowl appeared on the table. I shouted at her to go and catch a mouse. She dived into a cupboard, returned with the prescribed mouse which she gorged greedily, before resuming her demand for chicken. I had a great respect for Sabby and she taught me the basic fact of life that no man is master in a house which he shares with a cat. Sabby had one other weakness. She was the archetypal girl who couldn't say no. For the rest of her life she presented us with three litters of kittens a year. A neighbour took two of the kittens on the understanding that we would have them back if she ever emigrated.

On the day she left for New Zealand Lynda collected them and shut them in a barn thinking they would accept this as their new base. The male, Sooty, escaped in terror and returned to his old home to be met by the new incumbent, a large retriever. He disappeared for a week before being captured and brought back to Milldown. I had just returned from hospital so was allotted the task of nursing Sooty until he settled down. Together we sat, comforting one another and considering our changed circumstances, building up a trust in each other from which to face the world again.

Sooty was the first cat to follow us to Windmill Haeme. A large and handsome cat, his whiskers turned prematurely white with the trauma of the move which gave him a very distinguished look. It also led to him being referred to as 'the white-whiskered worrier'. Although he trusted us implicitly he never lost his fear of strangers and would retire to our bedroom as soon as the dogs barked or a strange car arrived on the drive. On a cold evening he would precede us to warm the bed and curl up amongst our feet. He was infinitely more effective than a hot water bottle or an electric blanket and his purring has been a great comfort when sleep is elusive.

This year we have acquired a school of goldfish in our pond. We were watching these one evening when Sooty, who had joined us, leant over and showed an excessive interest in them. Fearing he was about to take up fishing as a hobby, I gave him a small push. He overbalanced, swam the width and emerged looking very crestfallen and pathetic having learnt that a cat may look at a queen but not at a fish. The White-Whiskered Worrier was always the least energetic of our three cats so in the autumn rush of calving and drilling we were slow to notice when he gave up hunting and spent more time sleeping in the garage or the bathroom. Since either of us feed the cats on demand it took a little while to realise that he was not eating. We rushed to the vets who confirmed our fears that the condition was terminal and should be terminated. How I regret pushing him into the pond. It must have seemed very unkind coming from the person he trusted most of all but how often have I said when it's too late, 'How I regret not visiting him once more' or 'why didn't I make the effort to patch up our differences'.

Twenty-Four

Of Ducks and Death

1996

If you come across a bird's nest beside the road, either in a tree or on the ground, and the mother is sitting on the young or on the eggs, do not take the mother and the young. You may take the young but be sure to let the mother go.

Deuteronomy 22:6

A friend has mallards laying outside his study window. In season, he can lean out of the window and collect breakfast. He is probably breaking a dozen laws and regulations but it does not put the ducks off lay. Anyhow, he has it on higher authority that this is acceptable providing he does not touch the ducks.

For several years we have been visited every spring by a mallard duck with or without a mate. Usually she rears a flotilla of ducklings on our dirty water lagoon. According to all scientific theories this environment should be lethal to all known forms of life but our cheerful and hardy visitors appear to thrive in this unpromising nursery. Daily they leave their pond to invade the dairy unit to scavenge morsels of barley which have fallen from the mangers. With a dozen ducklings dining amongst two hundred cloven hooves in a highly congested cattle yard, it seems impossible for them to survive but I have yet to see one trampled.

If a domestic duck lays away and sits on eggs, she soon falls victim to fox or badger so we do not understand how the mallard escapes detection. When the family have left, the mother joins our ducks by day. At night we drive them all into the security of the pen but, after being shut in, she flies over the protecting wire to take her chance with nature who, so far, has smiled on her daughter. Doubtless in the wild many ducks are victims. All flesh is as grass, so death is a fact of life. All animals owe life a death and *homo sapiens* is no exception. Of course, partings are traumatic and untimely death is tragic, but is it not equally sad to see life not lived for fear of disaster? Our ancestors, like wild creatures, faced problems of survival from birth but they did not hide in their burrows in case the fox should be about. Many of the enemies they had cause to fear have been conquered by medicine and science. We accept a thousand rules and regulations to protect us from everything, including our need to think for ourselves. Are we in danger of becoming so protected that neither our minds or bodies respond to stimuli? Is life becoming an eternal cricket match which is bound to end in a draw because no-one is ever given out? Is this why one generation is obsessed with gambling while the next plays Russian Roulette with drugs?

+++++

Country children who grow up surrounded by birth and death often find it much easier to accept death than those who only hear of it in undertaker's speech of 'loss' and 'passing on'. We recently overheard a four year-old who had just been told of his grandmother's death passing on the message to the deceased's dog - 'It's very sad, Ginny, 'cos Grandma has died. Mummy's very sad and we're all sad. I expect you're sad 'cos Grandma can't look after you anymore but you needn't be too sad 'cos Daddy says I can look after you now'.

+++++

When I was young and learning my trade, I spent much time in the company of a man, fifty years my senior, who had worked with stock all his life. I regret to say that, full of the theories I had learnt at college, I did not always respect the wisdom which cannot be taught but must be acquired by living. Jack was convinced that our cows would never give of their best because we did not feed them a pout. It took me some while to discover what a pout was. Apparently it consisted of collecting a little of everything available which was acceptable to a bovine stomach, cutting it all into small pieces, mixing it very thoroughly and placing a large measure in each cow's manger. This all sounded a lot of work to the boy who was doomed to become the motive power behind the mangold slicer and the mixing fork. I thought of the feed tables I had studied at college. Since every ingredient contained a definable quantity of protein and carbohydrate, how could this be improved by cutting and mixing? In any case each cow is equipped with an excellent cutting and mixing system and does not have an overriding urgency to knock off in time to bike to the Young Farmers' Club dance.

Last autumn I was faced with the problem of feeding a herd of cows through the winter on an insufficient quantity of silage. The experts all assured me that the answer was a diet feeder. This is an expensive machine into which one places a little of everything available which is acceptable to the bovine stomach. It breaks it into small pieces, mixes it very thoroughly and deposits it into the communal manger. Apparently, because it is so well mixed, all the ingredients have to be eaten together – no more picking the ham out of the sandwich – and the time taken to pass through the cow's four stomachs is increased. This enables more nourishment to be extracted from the ingredients so the cows give more milk of higher quality. My son has taken to the system like a mallard to dirty water since the motive power is a 90 horse-power tractor. I am left to ruminate on the wise words of another elderly farmer for whom I once worked: 'The day I stop learning about farming will be the day they screw me down'.

TWENTY-FIVE

1996

You cruel rogues that come this day to borrow
A sum that's promised but not paid tomorrow;
That take like wasps the fruit that's on its way
Towards my mouth, and never fear my nay…

WH Davies

Why did the chicken cross the road? More to the point, why, having crossed the road and laid an egg in a carefully concealed nest, does it then let out a clarion call to every predator within a hundred yards of its accomplishment. Hen birds are generally clothed in drab colours supposedly to camouflage them when sitting on eggs. Why did natural selection not preserve the slight variation of silent chicken.

Our bantams are in full lay now and the Muscovy ducks are helping out, but we are fighting a losing battle trying to keep the family in eggs. At first the occasional egg had a hole drilled in it if laid in the open. The magpies and jackdaws had moved in for the season. Then whole eggs, even large duck eggs, would completely disappear. Four crows had turned vegetarian and were living on a diet of eggs. If we didn't leave an egg in the nest no more would be laid there; if we did it was stolen. In desperation I bought some china eggs and placed them in the nests. Next day they had been taken.

Our corvids are truly omniverous. I tried building kennels of bales around the favourite nest sites so the bantams have to crawl along a dark tunnel to lay. Any day I expected to hear a magpie singing 'Anywhere you can go, I can go quicker', because they can, and still the eggs were holed and eaten. It is expensive to lose eggs so I tried to trick the chicken with old golf balls. The hens were happy, also the crows. If by chance you should see a large black bird bouncing in twenty metre hops please notify Milldown Farm. Enter the US cavalry or rather second son with a shotgun. Two shots and a passing pigeon bit the dust, the crows moved out of range. Son eventually grew bored with the lack of action and decided it was lunch time, so did the crows. Lynda decided it was time to take a hand. She blew six duck eggs and used hypodermic to fill them with Polyfilla. The Polyfilla gave the eggs a natural matt bloom. The hens were totally convinced as were the crows. To date, apart from countless dozen bantam and chicken eggs, we have lost three pot eggs, six golf balls and five, very heavy, Polyfilla specials. Add to that the time we have wasted and it would have proved cheaper to feed the family on sturgeon eggs.

Another bird has been causing us some problems this summer - Ulysses the peacock. My late father-in-law had a thriving community of peafowl at Paddlesworth. Without his care and attention their numbers have dwindled to six males. In the spring a young peacock's fancy etc so we were not surprised to hear that the flock was reduced to five. We then heard that he had been intercepted on his way to Newington, possibly off to jump train through the Tunnel on his way to the land where peahens live. As he had been captured Lynda felt obliged to collect him and introduced him to our small flock. Our dominant male quickly made it plain that he was not welcome. After being bullied for forty-eight hours he disappeared and we feared he had moved out into the open and become a fox's dinner. A few days later a telephone call informed us he had moved to Ottinge. He was ignominiously bundled into a car and returned with his tail sticking out of the window. He now seems to have settled for a compromise. He spends his days at the farm and at dusk disappears into the gloaming to sleep half a mile away in a large ash tree. Milldown rings with the verbal battle he conducts with the resident male perched on the farmhouse roof. Those of a superstitious nature are advised to keep well away from the heart rending screams that reverberate through the night.

TWENTY-SIX

1996

Let not ambition mock their useful toil,
Their homely joys or destiny obscure;
Or grandeur hear with a disdainful smile
The short and simple annals of the poor.
Full many a gem of purest ray serene
The dark unfathomed caves of ocean bear;
Full many a flower is born to blush unseen,
And waste its sweetness on the desert air.

Thomas Gray

It is often said that holiday romances are bound to end in tragedy. Tragedy I found in plenty but not the unremitting gloom of ancient Greece, rather a Turner seascape depicting a courageous struggle against the overpowering elements, a ray of sunlight piercing the approaching storm clouds.

I first met Jane at her baptism at Easter 1840, an infant of some six weeks, the admired first child of Elizabeth Mortimer and her husband John, a master mariner. I know little of the next 16 years except that the family continued to live in the pleasant fishing village of Kingsweir and increased by the addition of Mary Ann, Maria and John William. I believe she spent much of her time helping her mother care for her little sisters and brother during the regular spells when her father was at sea. Then in 1856 his ship was forced to lay up in Dartmouth by the October gales. The kindly skipper invited Sam, a personable 19 year-old deck hand to his home. On such chance decisions the wheel of life revolves. Sam lost his heart to his captain's vivacious but wilful daughter and his feelings were reciprocated.

Jane and Sam had fallen in love as have so many teenagers before and since. Jane's parents were against the match. At 16, Jane was too young and life would be hard living off the wages of a deck hand who spent most of his life at sea. But Jane had great determination and was not the girl to let a little parental opposition stand in the way of her great passion. John and Elizabeth decided the best plan was to let the fire of love burn itself out and they were allowed to meet when the ship docked for Christmas. The young couple seized the opportunity and eloped to Guernsey. With the limited communication of those times it was easy for Jane to lie about her age and after the banns had been published they were married in St Peter's Church, St Peter Port on Saturday 8th February 1857.

About 140 years later on 9th June 1996, I sat in the church when the Eucharist was over visualising the scene. The bride clothed in the beauty of youth, her eyes aflame with the passion of love whilst even at that tender age the set of her jaw marked her as one who was not easily deterred from her purpose. The mild Guernsey spring blossomed into glorious summer and life was good. Sam found work in the harbour and the fit young Jane wore her pregnancy easily. Then the work on the harbour was halted for winter and Sam had to return to sea. Jane had to cease work and felt so alone when on Wednesday 26th November, Samuel Joseph first saw the light of day.

Jane could not go out to work with a tiny infant but she was determined to contribute to the family's meagre budget. She changed lodgings to 1 Arcade Steps, a four-storey house built into the cliffs which surrounded the old town of St Peter Port, where she was able to take in washing. The survey of 1861 finds her there with three year-old Samuel Joseph with Sam working away. Four years had taken their toll. Each day started with the climb of 100 feet up the steps to the new town with a heavy basket of clean linen and the return with more work. The house built into the rock was always damp, more so because the washing was endless. Young Samuel ate like a horse and Jane went hungry but the child must come first.

We last see Jane in November 1866. She is propped up on pillows begging her cousin's wife Sarah to care for Samuel until his father comes home. Her once lovely face has lost the bloom of youth, her arms are devoid of flesh, the skin stretched like parchment over the bones of her cheeks. Only her eyes still blaze but now with fever. She died of consumption on the 11th of that month, burnt out at 26 having given her all - for what?

Relaxing on the ferry returning home from Guernsey, my mind turned to a dozen healthy, happy young women, many of them around 26 years old. Half of them are mothers, some solicitors, teachers, secretaries and their male cousins mostly farmers. They all believe they live industrious useful lives, which I am sure they do, but Jane could tell them a thing or two about that. I don't know if you, Jane, would think it all worthwhile, but I'm sure they do, for without your struggle to keep Samuel alive for those first nine years, none of your great-great-grandchildren would have seen the light of day.

I had set out to Guernsey a week earlier to relax and, maybe, find out something of my origins. I had learnt much more than I expected. Thanks to the assistance of a local librarian I had discovered how to use a microfiche to follow the records through and trace my pedigree.

Of much greater significance I had come to appreciate as never before, what a tremendous debt I owed to my antecedents. History teaches us, as a community, of the achievements of leaders, warriors and inventors. How little it tells us of the struggles of those who kept the famous figures warm, clothed and fed. If Jane were remembered as frequently as her contemporary, Queen Victoria, could we as blatantly forget the million Janes who continue to struggle in continents where history is repeating itself?

If Jane had led a sheltered life and lived to be 100, I can imagine being taken as a small boy to visit a bedridden old lady who had no part in my world because she was so very, very old. I paid no such visit and so can only remember a 16 year-old bride and a young tigress fighting for her young. For so long had I laboured under the misapprehension that there were young people and old people. Thank you great-grandmother for teaching me that there are just people and some have been around for longer than others.

TWENTY-SEVEN

1997

Day breaks on England down the Kentish hills,
Singing in the silence of the meadow-footing rills,
Day of my dreams, O day.
I saw them march from Dover, long ago,
With a silver cross before them, singing low.
Monks of Rome from their home where the blue seas, break in foam,
Augustine with his feet of snow.

James Elroy Flecker

During lambing we are grateful for the help of several voluntary assistant shepherds. One of these, Becky, was surprised to meet a small and attractive animal by the sheep yards. Coming from Birmingham she is not used to the variety of life which inhabits Milldown. A call brought Lynda and Jill running to the scene. As she was describing her experience, an extremely handsome stoat re-emerged from under a water tank, approached to within four yards of the trio and sat on his haunches to inspect them. He eventually decided they were too large for lunch and returned to his stronghold. I now have a fair idea who decapitated one of our pea chicks in the autumn. I also realise why I have spent about £40 less on rat bait this winter. It seems strange that whilst our shepherdesses were excited by their encounter with this savage predator, had one of the rats which he has consumed approached in this fashion a total rout would have ensued.

In the past it was considered a great benefit to have a stoat or weasel resident in the stack yard to protect the harvest before threshing. After threshing the corn was often stored in the upper storey of a two storey building to allow for better ventilation and better protection against vermin. We had one such granary at Newington. At about 48 feet long and half as wide, there was room to store four wagons and an assortment of other pieces of equipment safe and dry on the ground floor. One corner of the first floor was boarded up for the shepherd's artefacts. This gave the whole storey a wonderful aroma with bags of feed from all over the world, ground nuts from Africa, cotton cake from America, soya from the Argentine, palm kernel from India but, best of all, the locust bean. This, not the wriggly jumping kind, we children were told by a visiting priest was the locust which John the Baptist ate with wild honey in the wilderness. We chewed the sweet beans and imagined them spread with honey. The wilderness had no terrors for us. The roof was supported by wooden columns, slotted to hold duck boards which could be inserted to make bays of different shapes and sizes to hold innumerable small or large parcels of grain. Those not holding grain were fortresses, castles, boats or anything an eight year-old imagination could conjure up.

What we did not appreciate at that age was how beautifully the whole structure was built. Every hand-carved joint constructed as perfectly for a farm store as though for a mansion or a cathedral. Each tenon a statement by craftsmen long gone that 'there is no such thing as good enough', each tile laid in hay to prevent snow drifting through and spoiling the grain. I felt the same sense of pride in a job well done when, twelve years later, I first carried a two and a quarter hundredweight sack up the wooden steps to the loft, a sense that at last I was one of the unbroken chain of men to build and use this part of the English countryside.

TWENTY-EIGHT

1997

Git away bye m'bonny lad
Gan oot gan oot gan wide,
Y've missed that yow that's lying down I bet she's been and gone and died...
Come inta me y'brainless hound
Sit down, sit still stay there I think I saw her blink an eye
Ye gods she's lambed a pair
She's up she's off the stupid bitch Gan oot then fetch her here.

Henry Brewis

I have four collies and often feel I have one good one. Jet to run round the outside of the field and lift the flock, Lindsay to bring them in and Mo to hold them in a corner. If a sheep and her lambs have escaped into a wood, Smartie will seek them out and return them. Of course, they have other attributes being always willing to join up with grandsons for a game of football or take anyone needing exercise for an entertaining walk. There is so much of interest that can be missed on a walk if not accompanied by a dog. Would you have smelt where a fox passed last night, seen the mouse hiding in a clump of grass, taken a bath in the water trough or found that stick in desperate need of throwing? Nevertheless I must admit that at times I have felt a touch of envy for the participants appearing in 'One Man and His Dog'. Mind you, I've had one or two dogs in my time that would have come close to that level, if only they had clicked lucky and had a different master. How do those philosophical shepherds accept the fact that Glen's mind is less on sheep than on the terrier bitch back home and still keep the language fit to show before the 9pm watershed.

A farmer was telling me recently how he had just lost a paragon of virtue after 12 years of faithful service. This dog would lift, fetch, shed, pen and probably sign the transport document for the market. He had just one vice, he didn't like people. He was fine with the farmer and OK with the farmer's wife but couldn't even be trusted out with their daughter who would have dearly loved a family pet. Of course, every cloud has a silver lining and when work piled up as sales reps came in like sheep escaping through an open gate, slipping the dog off his lead would always solve the problem.

The farmer heard of a man who bred collies for trials. Those not suitable for trial work were sold off, partly trained, for commercial work. He took his wife and daughter to select a suitable candidate hoping to obtain an animal with a better rapport with the family. His second mistake was to think that after involving them he could, if necessary, invoke the vendor's money back guarantee if the dog did not work for him. Dog and daughter immediately established a great relationship. Once the dog had settled in to his new home he was taken to show his paces with the sheep. The dog was sent away. He went at great speed, admittedly he failed to keep to the edge of the field, but at least he found sheep. Out of a flock of three hundred he selected three, which seemed to be to his liking, herded them into a corner of the field, and stood guarding them, wagging his tail and looking extremely pleased with his achievement. No amount of coaxing and cajoling would persuade him to abandon his captives or show any interest in the rest of the flock. Amongst his other attributes he had obviously read St John's Gospel and realised it was essential to find the one he deemed lost and ignore the ninety and nine which were saved.

This performance was repeated continuously over the next two weeks. By way of variety, the dog, who jumped like a National winner, occasionally hopped over a fence to select a few of the neighbour's sheep. He had been trained to do fancy things with five sheep and no amount of caressing, cajoling or cursing would induce him to take on three hundred. The farmer had come to regard the dog as a lost cause but to claim his money back he had to persuade his wife and daughter to part with their much-loved pet. One morning things had not gone well. The sheep had broken into the wheat. One had achieved its life ambition of dying in the middle of the corn where collection of the carcase would necessitate causing further damage. He had had to retrieve the miscreants with the minimum of canine assistance. He sent the dog off to round up the sheep for shifting to a safe field. The animals headed in the wrong direction. The farmer's patience snapped at last. Knowing it was useless to pursue on foot as George Orwell said 'four legs good, two legs bad', he gave chase in his Land Rover. As he drew level the dog turned straight into the truck. There was an almighty bang and panic seized the driver. Not only could he not claim back his money but, much worse, how could he explain to his daughter that he had just killed her adored pet. He leaped from his seat to see the victim struggle to his feet, shake his head in disbelief and stagger to his master wagging his tail. He silently made a reckless vow that the animal must stay even if he never worked again but, strangely, from that day he took to sheep like a collie should. Perhaps he felt that if he didn't pull his weight the truck would hit him really hard next time.

TWENTY-NINE

1998

Lead us, Evolution lead us
Up the future's endless stair;
Chop us, change us, prod us, weed us;
For stagnation is despair:
Groping, guessing yet progressing,
Lead us nobody knows where.
Wrong or justice, joy or sorrow,
In the present what are they
While there's always jam tomorrow,
While we tread the onward way?
Never knowing where we're going,
We can never go astray.

CS Lewis

Spring is coming. Thus says Lent and with it, if we still believe the promise of Genesis, the grass will grow, the seeds will germinate, the trees will burst into leaf, the birds will pour their souls through their throats proclaiming their pride in a nest full of the future. If tempted by the warmth and all this pristine beauty, you should chance to wander through the meadows, the visual appreciation will be enhanced by a bright yellow display of objects of a minimum size of 55mm wide and 45mm in length covered in black printing a minimum of 5mm high.

These will approach at escalating speed upon four legs. 'Be not concerned, they will not harm you', but will slither to a halt at the limit of your reach. No, I have not ascended to the dizzy heights of writing science fiction but, like all cattle farmers the balance of my mind may have been disturbed by the latest directive of the Ministry of Arable Farming and Foolishness. I apologise in advance for that printing error.

For months, even years, committees of 'experts' have pondered the problem of permanently identifying cattle. For the first time in 50 years farmers have been unanimous. Let us continue to use the small metal tags which fit tightly to an animal's ear, are virtually tamperproof and hardly ever become trapped and tear the ear in two. Many of us have tried using large plastic tags because they are easier to read at a distance and can hold more information. Unfortunately, the information is somewhat irrelevant when three tags are found in a hay rack or on a fence whilst three heifers race round a paddock showing three ears where two grew before. Is this a problem? Our experts are made of sterner stuff. Why are cattle equipped with two ears if not to wear one primary and one secondary gold medal. If only farmers would concentrate on their job of ordering, and paying for, expensive individually created, specifically numbered individual tags and replacing those lost within the, as yet to be ordained, time limit, the overtaxed experts could concentrate on policy.

Two months before D Day, the experts decide on a great concession to stop the farmers whingeing. Let them have metal secondary tags but order immediately because no dairy calf will be allowed to be born after the 1st of January 1998 unless two tags are available and fitted within 36 hours of birth. The tag manufacturers now think it timely to announce that they will not be able to meet their orders on time, so the committee of experts give a second great concession. Calves born to beef cows will not need to be tagged until they reach 30 days. Since most beef cattle produce calves in the field, after thousands of years practising, neither calf nor cow is too keen on human interference. If you think you can catch a 29 day-old beef calf, punch two holes in its ears, fit two tags and then reach the fence before its mother, just sign up for the next Olympics. Not only will you probably receive a gold medal of your own, but you will have a much better chance of living to draw a pension. As one battered and bruised beef farmer once told me 'If you have to help a Galloway calve, make sure before the calf hits the deck that you are half-way to the fence.'

One month before D Day and the EU decide they cannot accept metal secondary tags and issue an edict that farmers do as they are told and leave strategy to the Europeans. The local NFU recommend that Herr Fishley should be decorated - with a plastic tag attached to every conceivable appendage, more farmers cancel their tag orders and the manufacturers knock off for Christmas. Two weeks later, a deal is struck. I am not privy to the small print, but it probably involves damming up the Straights of Gibraltar and filling the Mediterranean with surplus olive oil, in return for which, the EU have agreed that we can use secondary metal tags which have not been produced by the end of January to tag calves born on the first of January within 36 hours of birth.

Back in the fifties I was taught a simple routine by a brilliantly clever vet. First deliver your calf, then clear its airways, swing it by its hind legs to take blood and oxygen to its brain, spray the navel to prevent infection, administer a hormone injection to assist the removal of the placenta, get the cow to her feet and teach the calf to drink. No wonder the public thought any fool could be a dairy farmer. 45 years on I learn that the first essential is to check the latest decision of the EU, the second to fix two tags to ears smaller than the tags and the third to record details of the calf and calving. Maybe the fourth should be to deliver the calf to the Hunt Kennels after it has died of an obstructed airway. Are we not fortunate to have committees of experts to worry about the difficult bits?

THIRTY

1998

Let not young souls be smothered out before
They do quaint deeds and fully flaunt their pride
It is the world's one crime its babes grow dull,
Its poor are ox like, limp and leaden-eyed.

Vachel Lindsay

As a child I was given a boys' book on TE Lawrence's exploits in, wait for it, and remember this publication is for reading before the 9pm watershed, Arabia. I also read the Daily Express, which was highly critical of illegal Jewish immigrants who were taking the lives of the British Peace Keeping Force. Not surprisingly, after studying the Merchant of Venice, I was convinced that Jews were bad and Arabs were good. I had to grow up before I learnt that life is not like that and anyone who commits themselves, body and soul, to any political doctrine needs a hide like a rhinoceros to deflect the arrows of truth which, sooner or later, will be hurled against them.

I suppose I started to mature when I was called up on national service. Our lives were brightened when we received food parcels from home, which were hidden in our lockers until we were on our own. One day a parcel arrived for Alan, the only Jew in our billet. He immediately shared it with all of us and suddenly all our lockers were open and we were tasting a whole range of cooking. It was then that I remembered that it was not a Christian, but a Jew who performed the original feeding of the five thousand. Some years later I sold a house to a Jew. He haggled over every fitting and detail. After the deal was completed I never visited him without being offered a glass of whisky, he gave me back most of the fittings he had argued over. Each year I was presented with an expensive diary and given a large box of fireworks for the village Guy Fawkes night. All this has little relevance to the trip which we took to the Holy Land in May except to say I believe I had a relatively open mind.

One could not fail to be impressed by the theological history stretching back to the dawn of man's time, but in a party consisting of one third priests I feel completely out gunned on this subject. At least I could claim to be the leading agricultural expert in the group. Driving from Tel Aviv to Jerusalem at the end of a long day my first impression was of a land flowing with milk and honey. The cows were there in large yards, covered against the heat of the sun. If the bees had gone to bed, no doubt they would be back in the morning. The land was flat, fertile, well farmed and highly productive. Then a subtle change occurred, we were climbing, at first slowly then more dramatically. Arable land gave way to fruit, then to forest, finally to scrub and then bare mountain. I was reminded of the drive through the fertile fields of Hereford to the peaks of Snowdonia except that the Welsh dragon always has a green background. Here a bare mountain meant just that.

We stopped on one of the hills surrounding Jerusalem. To our right arguably the most historic city in the world, but I could not stop my eyes from turning to the left. So this was the wilderness. For 50 odd years I had carried in my mind's eye a picture of an undulating countryside, dotted with scrub and patches of dried up vegetation, littered with rocks and the occasional mountain, it was all in those marvellous thumbnail sketches in the Good News Bible, but not this. This was just mountain, sand and rock, and then more mountain, sand and rock as far as the eye could see. How could even a fit young man survive for 40 days and nights in that searing heat? Of what could he eat or more important, drink? Still more mind blowing, how could a nation survive out there for 40 years? Tiny babies, pregnant mothers, small wonder that they wanted to turn back and make bricks for the Egyptians. Is this the basis of the obdurate resilience of the Jewish nation? An endurance forged in the heat of the Arabian desert. A boy came into view driving five goats around the foot of a mountain, so even yet there is life, although how it lives I can't imagine.

Over the week we saw many Bedouin camps, their summer homes a patchwork of goats' hair blankets, corrugated sheets and plastic draped over an assortment of any supports which would hold up a blanket. As we grew used to the scene we could spot the many caves in the limestone which provide winter quarters for man and animals. Doubtless their ancestors slung rocks at the Israelites who intruded onto their 'grazing'. What is 40 years to a people who have dragged a living from the wilderness for four thousand? During the day the women sit in the streets of Jerusalem selling goats' cheese and desert herbs. Oh to take our dairy inspector to Israel!

Of course the Bedouin are a separate people. I cannot imagine how anyone who was not born in the desert could survive under these conditions or indeed would want to. It appeared to me that most of the Palestinian Arabs dwelt in the Arab quarter of Jerusalem or in villages reserved for them. If they are needed to work in the Jewish quarter they are given a work permit which gives them rights of access by day, but not by night. Cars with a telltale P on the number are not allowed into the Jewish quarter at any time, 'It is necessary for security!' We stood on the walls of the house of Caiaphas and looked down on an Arab farm. A dozen chicken scratched around a two-storey building which appeared to house farm and family, a donkey stood, lost to time, three goats sniffed hopefully round a pile of rubbish. I thought of the cattle lots and broiler sheds around Tel Aviv, to which this had less resemblance than a shekel to a dollar. That is not surprising when one can guess the source of the money which financed the latter.

Later in the week we travelled to Galilee. Now I could really see what rich soil, capital and a guaranteed supply of water could achieve. Avocados, bananas, cotton, date palms, all grew in profusion alongside more mundane crops such as the wheat, barley, lucerne and sweet corn which you might see on Milldown. Even with these I was reminded of the sower whose seed brought forth a hundred fold, a feat which I have unsuccessfully been trying to emulate for 40 years. As a farmer, I appreciate more than most that crops like this do not just happen. Even with rich soil, capital and irrigation a lot of planning and sheer hard work are needed. Perhaps I was being unfair, that in less dedicated hands even these assets would have been wasted. We drove through a fertile valley bottom. On one side of the river the land heaved with rich crops, on the other rich grass stood tall and ungrazed. I was told the cropped side belonged to the Jews the uncropped to the Arab. I asked why the Arabs did not farm as the Jews and was told 'Security, it is close to the Lebanese border so it has been mined'. Am I too cynical to think that if there were no mines there would have been no water for irrigation either?

Jerusalem is an exciting and vibrant city even without its history where, even after many warnings, I very nearly succeeded in having my pocket picked. More clear is the memory of a little lad about six years old, who left his playmates by the side of the road and ran to hold my hand, walked with me for 20 paces, blessed me with a beautiful smile and rejoined his companions. What are his options ten years hence? What a waste that pickpocket or terrorist seem the most likely careers. Clearly there have been atrocities committed by both sides. I was told that the official view of the Jewish Orthodox Party is that they should persecute Arabs to avenge the holocaust. I pray my informant was wrong, but saw little evidence to prove it.

THIRTY-ONE

1998

Lynda Mary had a very little lamb!

We often say 'It is good to start the lambing with some bother to clear the trouble out of the way', which is another way of saying 'Accept the inevitable'. This year was no exception as the first ewe to lamb presented a large lamb backwards in the middle of the night with the inevitable fatal result. It is at such moments we are grateful that most of our relatives are in the business. The resident farmer's wife is hastily despatched to visit all connections in search of a foster lamb. There is no point in 'phoning first as any FW with a suitable candidate will be too busy feeding it to sit by the telephone.

When despatching a FW on such a mission it is advisable not to hold one's breath, or even expect other than bread and cheese for lunch. Deprived of normal communications each FW visited will contribute a horror lambing tale to the bush telegraph. In this case we heard of a farmer who was unable to manage a multiple birth and delivered the whole package to the vet. It was decided a caesarean was called for. The farmer returned home. In the morning the call came: 'Please collect sheep and three lambs as soon as possible.' Half an hour later he collected one ewe and three lambs; one alive, one dead and one dying. By the next morning the first lamb had joined his siblings. A cousin, whose wife was fed up with feeding a particularly obstreperous lamb, kindly offered a replacement, but was told he could have the ewe to feed the lamb and not to pay for her until she had completed the job. The sheep was delighted to receive a strong healthy lamb and mothered it instantly. Unfortunately, although she was built like a page three girl, appearances can be deceptive; she was all show and no milk. For the next two weeks she provided the lamb with TLC leaving the FW to feed it. On the morning the bill arrived from the vet the ewe decided to do what all sheep do best and left to join her triplets.

After this dire warning a suitable lamb was procured and for two weeks Shorn only left her cupboard and radiator to be fed and cuddled. Since she could initially only drink about one tablespoon full at a time, the times had to be very frequent and unhappily took priority over the feeding of the master of the house. After a few unsteady staggers around the kitchen she rapidly graduated to dancing round the kitchen with the collies, whom she adored. Mo, who had just had a litter of pups leave, reciprocated her feelings keeping the lamb washed and groomed. We even found Mo with her front legs on a chair so her adopted daughter could suckle her. She still regarded Lynda as Mum and would grow very excited at the sound of her voice. The chief objection to an indoor lamb came from the cats. Their protests became more vociferous as she developed a taste for cat food and would beg for this by picking up their dish and bringing it to us. This was ruled off limits and much to my disgust she was persuaded to eat porridge oats, my staple breakfast. Shorn was soon taking regular walks to the farm with Lynda and the collies, she was no trouble crossing the road as she copied the dogs in everything. Unfortunately she was afraid of sheep. Eventually, for reasons of hygiene, Shorn had to move to a garden shed, which caused several nights of bleating. She is now learning to share her shed and run with two orphans. She will be pleased to meet you at the Flower Festival, but don't mention mint sauce.

THIRTY-TWO

1998

They shall not come with warships
They shall not waste with brands
But books be all their eating
And ink be on their hands
What though they come with scroll and pen
And grave as a shaven clerk,
By this sign shall you know them,
That they ruin and make dark.

GK Chesterton

Once upon a time when a milking cow reached the end of her productive life and age lay heavily upon her she was transported to the local slaughter house and swiftly dispatched. Thereafter, depending upon her age and condition, meat was exported, pet food produced and the rest rendered down for glue or fertiliser.

Now, because it is reasonably easy to recognise that a bovine animal is over 30 months from its dentition, it is decreed that all above that age could pose a health risk and must be incinerated. A friend had three old cows in this category. They were loaded into a livestock box behind a Landrover and he set off for the abattoir. The day was windy. Driving along the slow lane of the motor way a foreign juggernaut passed too closely, creating turbulence which over turned the truck and box. The Landrover rolled twice then came to rest on the hard shoulder: miraculously the driver only suffered cuts and bruises. After turning over once the box sat, sans wheels, in the fast lane, its passengers still contained. The farmer walked back along the hard shoulder and retrieved his mobile, his guardian angel was on overtime, and 'phoned the police who closed the carriageway, and another farmer who came with Landrover and box. To their amazement the three cows walked out of their wheel-less transport apparently unharmed and loaded calmly into their new vehicle. They arrived late at their destination to be told that the ministry vet had left. There followed a delay whilst the official was contacted and persuaded to return so that sometime later he could make the official diagnosis that the animals were fit to be put down for incineration. It all makes work for the working man to do!

+ + + + +

We have recently been pet sitting for a family who are on holiday. We felt we had to decline the offer of two horses but agreed to watch over three very friendly, but noisy, collies, an appreciative pig and the most neurotic sheep I have ever met. Sheep was reared on a bottle, which usually leads to a lifelong acceptance of the human race. If this applies to Sheep she just does not appreciate that I am human. Every morning I had to let Sheep out of the shed she shares with Polly Pig to graze for the day. Polly is content to wallow in a small muddy yard. As I entered the shed Sheep shot out of the small door into Polly's yard. I am still trying to grasp how a sheep, resembling a small hippopotamus, can fit through a small door. I ran round to the back of the shed. Sheep squeezed back through the door and prepared to repeat the manoeuvre. After the third attempt I decided to bring into play the superior intellect of the human brain. I filled a bowl with pig/ sheep food and called Polly into the garden, she immediately followed. I think I must have a way with pigs or the food is very good. Sheep followed in a wide circle looking very wary. I led Polly back in the shed feeling very smug. As we walked through the door I was hit in the small of the back by 150lbs of flying mutton. I lay in the straw beside the pig, my face in the feed bowl, Polly was snuffling in my left ear, worried that I was eating her breakfast. The next time round I shut the door as the missile was fired and left a sheep shaking her head with all the appearance of a headache.

Two days later I was disturbed by a grandson hammering on the door. He told me the pig was at the farm and Lynda needed help to take it back. I was somewhat sceptical, knowing that grandson's sense of humour, but he was right. It took four of us to coax a tired Polly into our box. Sheep, who had followed her, took off in terror at the sight of the box, but fortunately met a member of her family coming to our assistance. As soon as he spoke to her Sheep followed him like a large woolly dog. I can only conclude that, since I was commissioned in June, to collect Sheep for her annual fleecing, Sheep is not as woolly headed as she appears, but possesses an elephantine memory. Next morning, at 7am sharp, pig and sheep arrived at the farm for breakfast and then returned, a round trip of a mile, on their eight cloven hooves. We haven't yet worked out how a pig, which had previously never wandered far from home, should unerringly locate the new food source, it could not have tracked us by scent as we always travel on wheels to prevent dogs following; in any case I resent being classed as a truffle.

The two older collies were quite happy to stay at home minding the house and garden. The hyperactive one, we had bred ourselves, or rather Lyndsey, who we thought old enough to know better, had unexpectedly produced one undersized pup, with sufficient energy for ten. She is an enthusiastic darts player, pulling the darts from the board and returning them for her opponent to try again. Nellie can climb like a monkey. She shows the true mountaineers' masochistic sense of fun, scaling our five-foot paling fence just for the pleasure of coming back the other way. Her courage cannot be doubted. When she is shut in the back of the truck she roars challenges at Bella the Alsatian and Jodie the Pyrenean offering to take them on together, but if she meets another dog in the open, like Macavity, Nellie isn't around! At the sight of a fowl her ears prick up and her nose starts to twitch, but so far she has resisted temptation. When she was born accusing fingers were pointed at Smartie. Today we have been watching her playing with Mo. Seeing her stalking through the long grass, ears pricked over russet face, brush carried low Smartie is now demanding a DNA test on a local fox.

THIRTY-THREE
2003

Prompt me, God;
But not yet. When I speak
Though it be you who speak
Through me, something is lost.
The meaning is in the waiting.

RS Thomas

One damp November Sunday found me returning triumphantly from Wales with two Huntaway cross Collies in the back of the car. We anticipated a noisy journey, but the dog guard we had borrowed proved superfluous, and the pups slept for most of the trip.

They were probably tired out after joining their brothers to show off their collective skills at keeping a couple of dozen rams in a tight lump. After seeing that the pups were enthusiastic and friendly and appeared healthy we had prepared to leave, only to discover that the last cheque in my book had already been made out. What a place to run out of currency, half way up a Welsh mountain on a Sunday morning. To my surprise I was assured that the general store/filling station in the nearest small village also served as a bank, seven days a week. How did we ever survive without plastic? Pups paid for and we were on our way.

I was not labouring under the illusion that I had the patience, time or the skill to train two pups for the price of one. As we left for Wales I had seen my brother, who said he could do with a Huntaway. Early next morning he was on the 'phone to confirm the order. Lynda, who was still loyal to the Border Collies which she had known and loved all her life, kept repeating tales of the skills and affections of friends long gone. She reminded me how her father's Judy was so attached to me that she interrupted our courting.

When taking my leave of Lynda, Judy would howl in jealousy so that the whole family knew what was going on. She reminded me that all our children had been taught to walk by the patient Cinders. She would stand over the toddlers, who could not resist sinking their fingers into the thick hair and pulling themselves to their feet. Then, if the child wanted to move the dog moved too. If the child wanted to stand they stood. Cinders was cuddly toy, walking frame and child minder all for the price of a few biscuits and an occasional pat on the head. I defensively pointed out that the pup in question was half Welsh Collie and proceeded to enumerate the almost super canine powers of my uncle's legendary 'Welshy'. My uncle had to repair a fence one morning before the cows were turned out to grass. He threw his coat on the grass and called 'on guard'. This told Welshy that she was not required on this task but she should stick around and not wander off. The day passed uneventfully enough until Uncle Jack opened the door of the farmhouse scullery to give Welshy her supper. Panic set in at the sight of no dog. Then mentally retracing the day's footsteps he set off in the moonlight in search of his coat. On the coat lay Welshy, supperless, but content that she was doing her master's bidding.

Conversation turned to a name. Most of our puppies are home bred and some little quirk of appearance or mannerism suggests itself. Two young visitors named 'Mo', because the white markings on her head reminded them of a Mohican haircut. Jef came straight out of Ambridge as Phil Archer had a new Collie at the same time as I did. I suggested Beulah, after the little Welsh village where she was born, but it was stated that Beulah was not a name. Nor was Florence until Florence Nightingale was born there. Casting my mind back 50 odd years I remembered a cousin who had a friend called Beulah. The discussion was closed and the pup had been named. Beulah was dropped in our back yard while we took her sister to my brother. As soon as they were parted they started to sing like the four and twenty blackbirds. I could not tell you the words of the song, but I CAN tell you that that song contained all the pent up sorrow of being taken from Mum and the entire world which was home.

The next week was spent learning her name and learning to come when called. Learning that when you come to your name nice things happen and when you don't you are growled at which is frightening. Meanwhile, back at the ranch I was learning a few facts of life. The first was that Huntaways have very powerful personalities. The second is they are wonderfully affectionate and would love to be praised for coming when called, AFTER they have finished what they are doing.

I suppose it is not only Huntaways or indeed dogs that fall into that category.

THIRTY-FOUR

2002

AG Street once wrote 'That however bad the British weather, the climate was sufficiently benign that, even in medieval times (*before shifting vast quantities of food around the globe became a practical proposition*) we never starved.' He went on to add that after a wet harvest the beer would be poor and the bread might be mouldy, but we would survive to try again next time. Regrettably there were individual casualties who slipped through the net of life, but the community as a whole carried on.

This of course did not apply in Ireland where, within the lifetime of men I have met, starvation has come close to destroying a community. Here the famine was brought about by potato blight, which followed the potato from the Americas via Belgium. The community was forced into the trap of relying on one crop for sustenance. There is no other crop which is suitable for growing in the north and west of Ireland that will produce as much energy as the potato. The best alternative is probably the dairy cow, (stop up your ears all cholesterol advisors) which is why dairy produce is their top export. She is in no way a quick fix option. Of course one swallow does not make a summer nor one Brent goose a winter. Even in the poorest places most will struggle through the first year. When the blight struck again people were forced to eat next year's seed to stay alive, so in the third year the area of crop was greatly reduced. There was little to eat and no money for the rent so the starving were forced to leave their homes to wander the roads seeking any support they could find. The welfare provisions, even for those times, were hopelessly inadequate and unequally applied. The Prime Minister repealed the protectionist Corn Laws to reduce the price of alternative foods, but cheaper foods were of little use to those with nothing at all. Many died of starvation and many more emigrated on the 'Fever Ships' heading for a new life in the New World. We can only pray that they found one.

What of this year's harvest? Of course I realise that living in a global economy my harvest has a negligible effect upon a local shopping basket. It is much cheaper to produce chicken joints in Malaysia where animal welfare is not an issue, wheat from Hungary where safety is not a problem or potatoes from Egypt where picking is cheap. However, since some of you have been kind enough to enquire I am able to report that, after last year's debacle, yields are reasonable and I only have the price to carp about. Wheat prices have dropped down to the level of the seventies, but in this we are extremely fortunate. If you notice next spring that my trousers circle my waist a little more easily it is less likely that I am on the verge of starvation than that the bread maker has broken down. In the meantime there are ten million people who could have starved to death.

As in Ireland there are numerous reasons contributing to this potential disaster, of which the first was over dependence on one crop which then failed. In this case it is reliance on maize and its failure brought on by drought, which followed floods in 2000. As Ireland suffered from absentee landlords so in Southern Africa politics increased the problem. Displaced farm workers are not allowed relief, if they support the opposition. The brother of a friend of mine was murdered for trying to produce food for some of the population. Some of the most fertile land in Zimbabwe is lying derelict while 45 000 farm workers swell the ranks of the starving. It would be easy to say, let those who have created the problem provide the answer, but they are not the ones who will starve.

This raises a new bogie. Whoever was blamed for the weather in 1845 it certainly was not global warming. If this is the cause of the erratic weather, which has created the problem, it cannot be dismissed as an act of God, but rather posted up as an act of man. If it is in fact an act of man, it is surely the responsibility for all of us who have contributed to pick up the bill. Would our season of harvest not be an appropriate time to replace some of the harvest, which is lost?

THIRTY-FIVE

2001

Out through the fields and the woods
And over the walls I have wended;
I have climbed the hills of view
And looked at the world, and descended;
I have come by the highway home,
And lo it is ended.
Ah, when to the heart of man
Was it ever less than a treason
To go with the drift of things,
To yield with a grace to reason,
And bow and accept the end
Of a love or a season?

Robert Frost

As I sit before a blank screen on a warm October morning it is difficult to remember that Christmas is just around the corner. How rapidly the years rotate in this millennium. Is it really 60 years since a whole lifetime separated next Christmas from the last? When one has waited for all that time you are ready to savour the last drop in the bucket. The fact that we were fighting a war which, to say the least, was not going well for us, could not detract from the glamour of the season. Rather because we accepted the austerity of everyday living, the tatty old paper chains and second hand presents acquired a special glamour. I have never tasted turkey more succulent than the big old cockerel whose clarion call no longer awoke us for school.

Ten years later my memories are more of work than play. Not that I worked unduly hard, but that I had left school and was part of the farm. It was one of my great pleasures to be the first on the scene in the morning, as a teenager with a busy social life, a pleasure more often missed than taken. If I did arrive first in the morning it was like entering a secret world. I would slide the door open a few inches and stand while the warm sweet breath from the cow shed drove back the frosty air of the early winter morning. I could hear an occasional shuffle and the gentle breathing of the animals nearest the door. When I switched on the light the unnatural change brought forth a mixed response. Those who were heavy in calf grunted a protest at the sudden disturbance while the recently calved members of the herd scrambled to their feet lowing for breakfast. We had stalls for 66, but one of these was often taken up by the bull. During the winter the cows were kept in their stalls all night and released for exercise during the day. Each knew her own place and usually stood patiently waiting to be tied in. In the winter there was usually a feed waiting in the manger. As in any community there is always someone who tries to beat the system for personal gain. Certain cows could be relied upon to grab a few bites as they passed a vacant manger and if the owner caught them a dispute would ensue. Two of us usually watched them in and tied them up. If a cow did head into a wrong stall by mistake a sharp 'No Freda' was generally sufficient to put her back on course.

There were five of us to cater for the needs of about 70 cows, a far cry from today when it is not considered economical to keep a cowman for less than 150. This was partly a legacy from the days when the milking was done by hand and 17 was a reasonable number for a milker to manage twice a day, but it also reflected a more relaxed way of life in the community as a whole. It was quite common to work at the same job for life. Pay levels were low, so no one worried too much how many hands were needed. The cow was king or rather queen, 'the lady that paid the rent'. If a cow lost the use of her legs after a difficult calving, there must be sufficient people around to keep turning her over until she found her feet again. Nowadays I fear that many cows are sacrificed on the altar of efficiency for lack of a little human muscle. This makes as much sense to me as driving staff to the limit so that they are burnt out and retire before 40.

It was standard practice to avoid any extra tasks on a Sunday morning so that we could have some time off. On Christmas morning it was traditional that the men, who did not have other stock responsibilities, would turn out to help with the cows. Some might be in particularly good 'spirits' from celebrating Christmas Eve with more enthusiasm than caution. There was much good-natured banter, the tasks were finished in record time and every one left in a good Christmas humour.

How different is the scene today. There may be two people in the modern dairy unit. They will produce an enormous quantity of milk, which will be sucked away by the tanker during the night and sold in the supermarket for less than bottled water. They may just have time to exchange a greeting. One is imprisoned in the milking parlour, the other in the cab of a tractor. This is progress. Of course we can't turn the clock back, but if Christmas isn't the time for nostalgia when is? Farming is no longer a social activity and I feel like the baby who was thrown away with the bath water.

THIRTY-SIX

1999

I remember, I remember,
The house where I was born,
The little window where the sun
Came peeping in at morn;
I remember, I remember,
The fir trees dark and high;
I used to think their slender tops
Were close against the sky:
It was a childish ignorance,
But now 'tis little joy
To know I'm farther off from Heav'n
Than when I was a boy.

Thomas Hood

Whenever I pay a post-Christmas visit to my grandchildren, or indeed any household including small people, I am overawed by the abundance of plastic flotsam which the giving season brings. It is not just that society as a whole is so much more affluent than it was 55 years ago; not even that electronics have advanced more in the last half century, than they had in the last two millennium. Surely the reason is social, rather than scientific.

When I was growing up, the adult world had just been pitched from a seemingly endless depression into a seemingly endless war. For a quarter of a century they had little chance to learn extravagance but they had learnt to make do with very little and to hold on to what they had. Perhaps it was easier for my generation than for our parents. We had never known abundance. We did not have to worry where the next meal was coming from, it always arrived and satisfied our voracious appetites. It was hard work slaying a dozen of the sheriff of Nottingham's men when your sword was two feet of roof lathe with a leaking enamel basin as a hand guard, but then arrows were of no avail against my trusty dustbin lid shield. Still I don't mind if I never taste another rabbit stew. Nowadays a toy sword is as large as life and twice as natural as the real thing. Not only does it look like high quality steel, with a jewelled handle for good measure, but it also hurls the insults and threats at its opponent, a trick we had to learn from Robin Hood himself.

If I had a toy car I regarded it as a plus if the wheels went round, and little short of miraculous if they turned in response to the steering. Today a toy car is expected to drive forward or reverse on command, turn left or right, flash its lights and make more noise than its full size role model. At seven, I treasured above all else, my collection of Britain's farm animals. These were irreplaceable and unique. Irreplaceable because metal was needed for tanks, not toys. Unique because there existed nowhere on earth another set like them. I had owned some of the animals from very early childhood. These were the ones which displayed the most unusual features. If I had inflicted damage, the first things to suffer were the legs. One leg was not too serious a problem as it could usually be replaced by part of a wooden meat skewer secured with elastoplast. A spot of enamel paint and Daisy was all set to re-join the herd to be milked in the restored Noah's Ark which served as a cowshed. If a more total disaster should strike a cow or, Heaven forbid a cart horse, all was not lost since partial amputation of the remaining limbs would usually allow a Dexter cow or a cob to rise Phoenix like from the ashes of tragedy. A pig, which once suffered injuries sufficiently severe to have sent my father's sow to the hunt kennels spent, with the aid of a daub of plasticine, the rest of his life happily wallowing on the cake drum, which served as a farm pond. Less fortunate, the cow whose legs were too short even for a Dexter, condemned to spend eternity as 'Down with milk fever'; a warning to all that even model farms were not beyond the 'Slings and arrows of outrageous fortune'. It certainly did not occur to us that it was politically incorrect to name by a physical defect. We named our animals, as our ancestors had their rulers and neighbours; Edward Longshanks, Richard Hunchback and Squint Jacob. We called our grey mare Waxnose and a black cow Wonky.

It did not occur to us to badger our parents for toys. We knew they were simply not obtainable, but there was just one chink of light shining through the curtain. Surely even Hitler could not control Father Christmas; and he didn't. It was years before we realised that it was an uncle and aunt and two older cousins who cleaned up outgrown toys and packed them into exciting parcels for our stockings. We did not need to browse through an Argos catalogue to whet our appetites for Christmas Eve, the excitement of anticipation, fed on exclusiveness, was almost too much to bear.

So when I wade, ankle deep, through a plethora of expensive electronic toys and exact models I certainly do not envy the children who own them, much less the parents who spend hours thinking of something different to really make this Christmas special by stretching their credit cards to the limit. Rather nostalgia and a profound sadness creep over me; regret that today's children never have the joy of owning something they really treasure, for in a world where everything has a price and nothing a value, none of their expensive toys are irreplaceable. I ponder that when Elham's own marathon runner was training for London he did not sit in his armchair conserving his energy, but toiled up and down the lanes. Will our children ever have the chance to develop their imagination to the full if, blackmailed by advertising pressure, all their requirements are catered for. No runner; I pensively sunk into my chair. Something jabbed me in the back. I cursed as I fished out a forked piece of elder about eight inches long. It was just the kind of revolver I always kept at hand when I was seven; just in case a burglar or stray wolf came in when I was alone. All, I see or rather feel, is not lost.

THIRTY-SEVEN

1999

We look before and after,
And pine for what is not:
Our sincerest laughter
With some pain is fraught;
Our sweetest songs are those that tell of saddest thought.

Shelley

When we moved to Windmill Haeme we were amazed at the number and variety of small song birds who shared our plot with us. Of course this was partly due to the quality of building site which surrounded our home and which contained every imaginable weed providing a continuous variety of food.

Farmers are seldom renowned as the greatest of gardeners. Gardens usually demand instant attention at the same time as the farm, so it took the resident Farmer's Wife several years to bring our plot under some sort of control. By the time this was achieved we had lost our choir of linnets and our charm of goldfinch, but still enjoyed a varied selection of visitors. We were delighted, last summer, when a pair of black birds nested in the pyracantha by our front door. All went well until the chicks fledged and then they vanished. Fortunately, like Robert the Bruce, the adult birds tried and, to our surprise, tried again, in spite of our efforts at keeping the cat in at the critical time all was in vain. No young birds survived. By now it was obvious that the culprits were our resident comedians, a pair of magpies. They had to go. This decision was confirmed when I was authoritatively told that a pair of magpies, rearing two broods in a season, will account for 250 song birds. At first I found this figure hard to accept but, on reflecting that this is only one egg or nestling a day for 125 days per bird, I resolved to reduce the local population of pies.

Doubtless this will put me in the wrong with one member of the editorial team who has a laissez-faire attitude to these problems, believing that, since it is in the natural order for herons to eat fish, it is acceptable for them to eat her goldfish. The blood of my gamekeeper grandfather flows too strongly in my veins to adopt this philosophical approach. I feel compelled to weigh in to help preserve the balance of nature, small though my influence can be. In the past the influence of keepers was much greater and doubtless their control of predators helped to maintain a heavy population of songbirds in the first half of the century.

Four or five years ago we had a visit from the South East Ayrshire Club. As we walked amongst the cows we could scarcely hear them moo for the sound of larks overhead. Our visitors, all country folk, were as impressed by our heavenly choir as they were by the cattle. Last year, when Elham School walked across the same field, I heard just two larks. The same herd of cows grazed the same grass; no sprays had been used, in general the management remained the same, so why the change? Larks nest on the ground. I have witnessed, from a first floor window, what happens when a badger comes across a coop and run housing a bantam and chicks. The first blow removed the protective run, the second floored the mother, attacking in vain to defend her chicks. One bite removed her head and left the intruder free to hoover up the babies before carrying the warm body back to her young.

This is not a comment on the morals of two animals, but rather a statement as to what occurred when two females followed their instincts to advance their species. The moral of the story is, if you want to breed poultry in the bad(ger) lands, be like the third little pig and build the house of brick. Larks do not have this option and are extremely vulnerable to a dozen snouts scouring their nesting sites night after night. So if governments bow to pressure from the tabloids and animal pressure groups, who have neither the wit nor will to think the thing through, and bring in stringent protection measures for one species, they should be prepared to undertake necessary control measures themselves. Alternatively perhaps, they should make one more adjustment to the education programme and insist that farmers are made responsible for teaching resident badgers to read the laws protecting nesting birds. It would be scarcely more bizarre than some of the edicts in my mail.

+++++

Any one viewing Country File on 10th April will appreciate the danger of clipping cattle before slaughter. Early in March I came to realise that it does not need anything as large as a fully grown bullock to impart considerable discomfort. Before lambing, sheep become highly vulnerable to twin lamb disease; the ovine form of pregnancy toxaemia. This can be brought on by a change in the weather, a change in the diet, or a sheep's perverse preference to die rather than live. The animal becomes low in blood sugar and attempts to produce it from its own reserves. It is then poisoned by the waste products which causes loss of appetite, which lowers the blood sugar, enabling the sheep to achieve its heart's desire of foiling the shepherds attempts of keeping it alive.

I had one such animal in the early days of March. She, with 30 mates, was busily stodging a field near the Nailbourne to mud chowder. My only hope of thwarting her ambition was to administer a pint of a patent remedy containing molasses and stimulants. I set out to feed the little flock with a bag of oats; cunningly concealing in my pocket a bottle of medicine. As planned, the sheep forgot that she was off her food and rushed to the trough with the others. In the melee I was able to grab my intended victim round the neck with my right arm, and holding the bottle in my left hand I attempted to remove the top with my teeth. Sensing a lack of concentration, my opponent swung round and hit me in the back of the knees with all her 140 pounds. Inevitably I landed on my back with a sickening slurp, but refused to relinquish my hold on sheep or bottle. Unable to break off the engagement, and seeing that I was taking it lying down, my adversary decided to do the same, right across my stomach. After trying to regain my breath for a couple of minutes I conceded there was no way of recovering from this position with patient and medicine so I reluctantly released my intended prisoner. She did not, as expected, immediately make good her escape but lay, contentedly ruminating, on the driest spot in the field. I found it quite impossible to move her, and was settling down to wait for someone to pass along the footpath when my oppressor grew bored with the game and ambled off.

The resident farmer's wife knows I am extremely attached to the land and is not unaccustomed to me returning with a fair amount of it attached to me, but even she felt this required some explanation. I told her my tale and wished she had been there to assist me. 'Yes' she replied 'with my video camera'. So much for a sympathetic ear.

THIRTY-EIGHT

ELHAM SCHOOL GO FARMING

1999

When I realised that the day I had invited a party from Elham School to visit Milldown was my wife's birthday, I thought, 'Woops, I've done it this time'. I believe, when Mr Fielding asked who would like to join the visit, and classes 2, 3 and 4 all volunteered, he probably thought 'Woops, I've done it this time'. Fortunately Lynda thought it might be rather fun to have 90 guests to celebrate the day with a BYOG picnic and being an eternal optimist never considered rain as a possibility.

Planning the route took a little thought, to avoid treading down standing fields of wheat, or running the risk of an unskilled driver coming suddenly upon 90 walkers. We finally settled on a devious two mile climb along little used footpaths. The rest we had to leave to the weather, and the genie of the farm, to provide such entertainment as it would.

The day dawned cool and clear. Cool was definitely in our favour with that climb ahead of us. At one high point we had to cross two stiles in quick succession. Have you ever thought how long it takes for 90 people to clear two stiles, especially when the stiles are high and most of the people aren't? Fortunately, by this time, the course had slowed even the most ebullient of tearaways to a stage where even they were beginning to notice their surroundings. As we stopped, in a set-aside field to look for signs of badgers, an enormous hare broke cover and ran right through our party. I knew then that the spirits of the country side approved of our visitors, and all we had to do was sit back and ride the crest of the wave. A group of lads found two leverets hidden in the grass and sharp eyes spotted several nests of field mice. Teachers were hard pressed fielding questions on wild flowers and grasses. Later on, Amadeus, usually a little stand offish with strangers, gave pleasure in coming to greet us whilst the dairy herd showed they realised the importance of the occasion by joining us *en masse*. Buzz the Welsh pony and Gail the sock lamb always love visitors, they might bring food you know, and the peacock showed his approval by displaying his tail.

I know all this really happened, because it is recorded in the wonderful thank you letters we received afterwards. These, the demonstrations by the JCB loader, the explanation of how the milking parlour worked, were all quoted as the favourite parts of the visit, but the one which received most votes was having a picnic lunch in our garden. To be fair it wasn't just the food, even after that long walk, I quote one letter of many, 'Whilst I was eating lunch I could see Elham from up there with its church poking out of the green trees. I was amazed at all the colours of the distant fields, together they look like one huge patch work quilt'. How good it is, at times, to see the familiar through fresh eyes. What fun we all had that day, and what a birthday party.

THIRTY-NINE

1999

Let not ambition mock thou useful toil
Their homely joys, or destiny obscure
Nor grandeur hear with a disdainful smile
The short and simple annals of the Poor

Gray

One of the drawbacks of modern mechanised agriculture is that there is no one to talk to any more. Looking back half a century work was much more fun. True it was very much harder and poorly paid, but this served to induce a Battle of Britain mentality in those who suffered together. We seldom worked alone, and a gang could curse weather, the wickens or the thistles much more effectively than one. To a teenager, sorry no such animal existed, to a boy learning his trade the meal breaks were an education. Just by sitting there and listening he not only learnt the virtues of good practice, and the penalties of bad, but the whole ethos of country life as it existed then. Into this debating chamber poured the combined wisdom of skilled craftsman, itinerant casual worker, employer and callow youth.

All this was much on my mind when I recently attended the funeral of one of the men I worked with all that time past. I was recalling some of the stories he had told me as we had toiled at tasks which occupy the muscles, but leave the mind and tongue free. I was told how he, the second child of seven, had come with his parents as lodgers to live with a family of six in a three bed room cottage. I was stopped by his amazed granddaughter who had heard nothing of this before and asked how they all slept. Another member of our old gang took up the tale and explained that the parents had a small bed, the baby slept in a drawer whilst the other six shared a double bed, three at each end. At the time the family lived off what the parents could earn from casual farmwork supplemented, as there were no welfare payments at that time, by catching moles at sixpence a tail. Each morning the son had to walk a round trip of three miles to collect stale bread, their staple diet, from the bakers before attending the local school. It all sounded like a nightmare from a Catherine Cookson melodrama, a tale from the middle ages, or a story from the third world. The granddaughter, reasonably well off with her own house, was aghast that her ancestors had to live like this within living memory.

This situation is not unique. Before the days of social security the death, defection or disablement of one or both parents could quickly bring a family to the gutter. I count myself most fortunate that my family have not suffered such misfortune in this century. 50 years earlier our chances of survival seemed slim. Great grandmother Jane died at 27, a victim of tuberculosis, the consequence of bad housing and malnutrition. Her husband followed, drowned at sea, a few years later, leaving my grandfather, a 12 year old orphan. He ran away to sea and shipped up in London as have so many runaways before and since. He slept in a lodging house with other lads working on the trams. They had to sleep with their boots on to prevent the rats biting their feet in the night. He was befriended by two families, whom he served as gamekeeper and eventually became a farmer. I owe an unpayable debt to these ancestors whose tenacity and endurance gave me a life, and the chance to do something with it.

Another great grandfather, John, was I believe born in the south west tip of Ireland, just before the potato famine. He too travelled to London, but with a parent. Facts are hard to establish with Ireland in such terrible turmoil, but it is much to their credit that they survived at all. He finished up in Maidstone as a chimney sweep. His daughters idolised him and my grandfather said, 'He was a jolly nice chap when he was sober, but he wasn't often sober'. Perhaps if he wasn't in continual pain from the cancer brought on by the soot he would have been sober more often.

I have many other ancestors whom I would love to meet and 'Have a one to one with'; the Sussex yeoman who was the first in the county to use a steam plough, the blacksmith's apprentice who married his master's widow and established one of England's noble families which produced, arguably, our greatest soldier statesmen since Sir Walter Raleigh and a Sussex publican who could tell me if he really did 'get away with murder'. If I could meet just two I think it would have to be great grandmother Jane and great grandfather John Attridge. I couldn't cure him, but a few pints of the black stuff might help him forget his pain.

Of course we all have ancestors, known or unknown, to whom we owe everything. Generally there is nothing we can do about that. Is it not a little unnerving to imagine how tough it could have been within the lifetime of those we can remember? If so can we do justice to ourselves if we shut our minds to the Johns and Janes of the world today? It is particularly appropriate, at Easter, to offer new life to those without hope as generously as we can.

FORTY

2003

'Well we didn't quite make it'. The comment could have applied to anything, but in this case it referred to our diamond jubilee. Not that Lynda and I had not been together for 60 years, although it is true we had not, but after 59 years we had sold our pedigree Ayrshire herd. In 1944 my father took a train to Shoreham and purchased four pedigree heifers. In 2003 Lynda and I drove down to Cornwall to see 38 in calf heifers auctioned off. Two short sentences which, to me, sum up the work of the last 44 years. The herd grew by selective breeding and a few judicious purchases.

In the late fifties, the herd, which had grown to around 60 cows and as many young stock, was decimated by tuberculosis. One of the original four cows was an undetected carrier. Because she was such a wonderful foster mum and would feed any calf given to her, each calf was started on her. So Shoreham Consistent (her name) wiped out most of a year's crop of calves. The government had launched the attestation scheme whereby all cattle had to be tested and those reacting to the test had to be slaughtered. We were left with 22 milkers.

In 18 years this had grown to 200. By present day standards the experts would tell us this is the minimum number for an economical dairy herd. They would probably add that they should be kept in an area with 40 inches of rainfall within a 20 mile radius of a cream factory. My brother and I decided to go our separate ways, each with his 100 cows. I have heard people launch an attack on Islam because the Koran allows a man to have four wives at the same time. Surely if a man's heart is so small that it cannot care enough for five wives, how can anyone love more than 100 cows. To bring the best out of a dairy cow one must love her as a child. Some are easy to love; they are responsive; they give of their best with but little encouragement. They do not misbehave to gain attention. Others are born disruptive. Perhaps they have a low boredom threshold and are fed up with the routine of milking two or even three times a day.

Most of our Ayrshires had been sold last year. The last 38 remained, the last calves from the dairy herd. Fortunately Elmo, our Aberdeen Angus bull, had not read the Koran so they were all due to calve this autumn. We knew that there was no trade for dairy heifers in this area since in so many of the counties dairy farmers had given up. We decided to take a holiday in the south west to spy out the land, where the situation was entirely different; many dairy farmers were turning to organic production. The smaller, hardy Ayrshires, with their broad 'lawn mowers' to eat grass rather than cattle cake, are ideal for the job. We were introduced to a dairy auctioneer, who travelled from Cornwall to Kent to check that 'Our Girls' were right for the job. He then found a haulier with a lorry big enough to take 38 expectant mums.

Two days before the sale the 'phone rang. We had a haulier who claimed he had the biggest lorry in the west. Did we have the roads to match it? Were there any low bridges on the road to the farm? I assured him that my son had driven a large combine past the farm that afternoon. He did not seem totally convinced, but said he hoped to be with us by midday. His daughter 'phoned at 11.50am to say they were at Newington. We had been advised to keep the heifers in overnight with just a light feed of straw. By now Lynda and I felt as if we should have taken the same advice. We walked slowly up to the farm collecting our eldest son who had volunteered to help with the loading. We heard a diesel engine in the distance, it grew closer, then turned and died away. At that point a Cornish haulier appeared over the brow of the hill, minus his cattle truck and daughter. The truck had been captured by a low flying oak tree and was going nowhere until we paid the ransom of a man with a chain saw. My heart sank. There was a 200 yard stretch of trees between the truck and the top of the hill. Lesson number one, never judge a truck by its width alone. I 'phoned younger son, who had just started combining a field of wheat three miles away, for assistance. The haulier returned to reinforce his daughter who was having a hard time persuading an impatient driver that a road blocked meant a blocked road. Lynda and I took turns at diverting the traffic expecting to descend the hill. Second son arrived and started to cut his way through the jungle which festooned the top of the lorry. Kevin, a neighbour who could not pass, climbed on the top to pass down the pieces of bough. Lynda stopped a police car seeking to descend the hill. The occupants told her that she could not stop them; it was their job to stop her. They could see that we were doing all that could be done, so after a little more banter they left us to it. I suspect that they had been summoned by an impatient motorist. Strange how some people think that a little bad temper will always oil the wheels. Inch by inch the truck rolled forward until it finally burst through. The driver's daughter opened the gate of the yard and cried out 'They've all gone, where are they to now'?

Sure enough there was not a heifer to be seen. For the past few days they had been shut in by night and turned out about 11am. Cows are creatures of habit, bad habits if given any encouragement. Having waited patiently for an hour they decided enough was enough, it was time for lunch. The gate was little impediment to the united efforts of 19 tonnes of beef, but I was humbled by the knowledge that this had kept them in all winter. Fortunately they obligingly stopped to mow off the first patch of grass which they located. We surrounded them and drove them back into the yard. What's quarter of an hour when you're already two hours late. We started to load, four small ones first.

One of the four decided this was not for her, so we found a replacement. Lynda informed us that the reluctant traveller was Lovely's twin daughter 514. We carried on loading without her, putting four or five in a pen. We were pleased to note they seemed to settle quietly in their pens. The haulier and his daughter certainly knew their job. At last there were only four left to go, including 514. Soon there was only one. She did not struggle or try to break away, she just stood at the bottom of the ramp, her body language stating, 'I live here and I'm not going away.' Second son reappeared on his way to the combine. With six of us pushing and shoving we started to gain just a little each time. Finally we shut the tailboard. The truck was about to move off when Kevin rushed in. He had lost his mobile. He was sure he had it when he joined us. If it was on the road it was sure to have been flattened. Suddenly a voice called down from the top of 'the tallest lorry in the land'. Second son had found it hidden amongst the leaves and twigs. How long would it have stayed there? The lorry moved off at 3:30 pm.

We followed an hour later feeling a little worn to be starting a 250 mile journey. The first 150 were trouble free, then as the light began to fade so did our clutch. When we ran into a gentle drizzle we discovered that one of our windscreen wipers, unused for so long, was disintegrating. It was with some relief that we reached our destination and saw that we could leave the market foreman to give the heifers bed and supper. All turned out well in the end, though there had been times when I had wondered.

+++++

POSTSCRIPT

Peter Vincent finished writing these Parish Magazine articles in 2006, and the foregoing is a selection of the whole. By then he had semi-retired from farming and was coping with health problems, particularly Parkinson's Disease, but the farm, and his family, remained central to his life. He died on 5th November 2010 and this booklet is a testament to his commitment to farming life and to the village of Elham.

Illustrations by

The Vincent Family

Gemma Wheeler

Patrick Wheeler